Georgia
Algebra
EOC

SUCCESS STRATEGIES

**Georgia EOC Test Review
for the Georgia End of
Course Tests**

Need more help? Check out our flashcards at: http://MometrixFlashcards.com/Georgia

TABLE OF CONTENTS

Top 15 Test Taking Tips

1. Know the test directions, duration, topics, question types, how many questions
2. Setup a flexible study schedule at least 3-4 weeks before test day
3. Study during the time of day you are most alert, relaxed, and stress free
4. Maximize your learning style; visual learner use visual study aids, auditory learner use auditory study aids
5. Focus on your weakest knowledge base
6. Find a study partner to review with and help clarify questions
7. Practice, practice, practice
8. Get a good night's sleep; don't try to cram the night before the test
9. Eat a well balanced meal
10. Wear comfortable, loose fitting, layered clothing; prepare for it to be either cold or hot during the test
11. Eliminate the obviously wrong answer choices, then guess the first remaining choice
12. Pace yourself; don't rush, but keep working and move on if you get stuck
13. Maintain a positive attitude even if the test is going poorly
14. Keep your first answer unless you are positive it is wrong
15. Check your work, don't make a careless mistake

Real and Complex Number System

Real, natural, whole, integer, rational, irrational, imaginary, and complex numbers

The set of real numbers contains all numbers which have distinct locations on a number line. Natural numbers are real numbers used for counting: 1, 2, 3, 4, ... The set of whole numbers includes the counting numbers along with the number zero: 0, 1, 2, 3, 4, ... The set of integers includes whole numbers and their opposites: ..., -4, -3, -2, -1, 0, 1, 2, 3, 4, ... Rational numbers include any real number which can be expressed as a fraction in which the numerator is an integer and the denominator is a non-zero integer; rational numbers include integers, fractions, terminating, and repeating decimals. Irrational numbers, such as $\sqrt{2}$ and π, are real numbers which are not rational; in decimal form, these numbers are non-repeating and non-terminating, so any decimal (or fractional) representations of irrational numbers are only approximations. The set of imaginary numbers includes all numbers whose squares are negative and therefore excludes any real number; the imaginary number i is defined as the square root of -1. The set of complex numbers encompasses both the real and imaginary; a complex number can be written in the form $a + bi$, where a and b are real numbers, and i is the imaginary number.

Below is an example of a diagram which shows that natural numbers are a subset of whole numbers, which are a subset of integers, which are a subset of rational numbers. All of these together with irrational numbers comprise the set of real numbers. Complex numbers include both real and imaginary numbers.

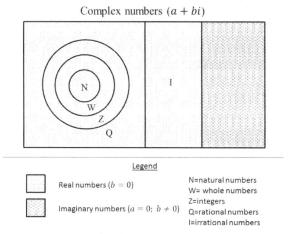

Complex numbers $(a + bi)$

Legend

Real numbers $(b = 0)$

Imaginary numbers $(a = 0;\ b \neq 0)$

N=natural numbers
W= whole numbers
Z=integers
Q=rational numbers
I=irrational numbers

Note that the sizes of the boxes and circles do not reflect the sizes of each set. Each set contains an infinite number of elements.

Example problems
Problem 1: Classify each of the following numbers as areal, natural, whole, integer, rational, irrational, imaginary, and/or complex.

$$\pi$$
$$-6$$
$$22$$
$$i$$
$$\frac{2}{3}$$
$$2 + 3i$$

π is an irrational number, a real number, and a complex number

-6 is an integer, a rational number, a real number, and a complex number

22 is a natural number, a whole number, an integer, a rational number, a real number, and a complex number

i is an imaginary number and a complex number

$\frac{2}{3}$ is a rational number, a real number, and a complex number

2+3i is a complex number

Problem 2: Determine whether each statement is true.
All natural numbers are real numbers.
Some integers are whole numbers.
Imaginary numbers are not real.
No integer is irrational.
All rational numbers are integers.

1. True; all natural numbers are real numbers.
2. True; some integers are whole numbers. Not all integers, however, are whole numbers, but all whole numbers are integers.
3. True; imaginary numbers are not real.
4. True; no integer is irrational. Integers are part of the set of rational numbers, and irrational numbers are not rational.
5. False; all rational numbers are NOT integers. All integers are rational, but not all rational numbers are integers.

Properties

Example problem
In the statements below, * and _ represent undefined operations. Name the properties illustrated in each statement and define for which operation(s) * and _ each of these statements is true. Also, identify for which sets of numbers these properties are true.

$$a * b = b * a$$
$$a * (b * c) = (a * b) * c$$
$$a * (b\_c) = a * b \_ a * c$$
$$a * b = a$$

1. $a * b = b * a$ illustrates the commutative property, which is true for any complex numbers a and b when * represents addition or multiplication.

- 4 -

2. $a * (b * c) = (a * b) * c$ illustrates the associative property, which is true for any complex numbers a and b when * represents addition or multiplication.
3. $a * (b\_c) = a * b \_ a * c$ illustrates the distributive property, which is true for any complex numbers a and b when * represents multiplication and _ represents addition or subtraction.
4. $a * b = a$ illustrates an identity, where the quantity a is unchanged by the operation * with the quantity b. This property is true for any complex number a when * represents addition or subtraction and when $b = 0$. This property is true for any complex number a when * represents multiplication or division and $b = 1$.

Note: The operation * can also represent "to the power of" when a is any complex number and $b = 1$ since, by definition, any number raised to the first power is that number.

Example problems

<u>Problem 1</u>
Simplify

$$i^{12}$$
$$(2i)^8$$
$$(-i)^{25}$$

Notice the pattern that emerges when i is raised to consecutive natural number powers:

$$i^1 = i$$
$$i^2 = -1$$
$$i^3 = i^2 i = (-1)(i) = -i$$
$$i^4 = i^2 i^2 = (-1)(-1) = 1$$
$$i^5 = i^4 i = (1)(i) = i$$
$$i^6 = i^4 i^2 = (1)(-1) = -1$$
$$i^7 = i^4 i^3 = (1)(-i) = -i$$
$$i^8 = i^4 i^4 = (-1)(-1) = 1$$

The imaginary number i raised to any whole power n is always $i, -1, -i,$ or 1. To find i^n, either continue writing the pattern $i, -1, -i, 1$ to find the nth number in the pattern, or, more simply, use properties of exponents to rewrite and simplify i^n.

$$i^{12} = (i^4)^3 = (1)^3 = 1$$
$$(2i)^8 = (2^8)(i^4)^2 = (2^4)^2(1)^2 = 16^2 = 256$$
$$(-i)^{25} = (-1)^{25}(i^4)^6(i) = (-1)(1)^6(i) = -i$$

<u>Problem 2</u>
Determine the values of a and b for which $\sqrt{a} \cdot \sqrt{b} \neq \sqrt{ab}$.

$\sqrt{a} \cdot \sqrt{b} = \sqrt{ab}$ when either a or b is positive or when both a and b are positive. For example,
$\sqrt{25} \cdot \sqrt{4} = 5 \cdot 2 = 10$ and $\sqrt{25 \cdot 4} = \sqrt{100} = 10$, so $\sqrt{25} \cdot \sqrt{4} = \sqrt{25 \cdot 4}$;
$\sqrt{-25} \cdot \sqrt{4} = 5i \cdot 2 = 10i$ and $\sqrt{-25 \cdot 4} = \sqrt{-100} = 10i$, so $\sqrt{-25} \cdot \sqrt{4} = \sqrt{-25 \cdot 4}$.
However, $\sqrt{a} \cdot \sqrt{b} \neq \sqrt{ab}$ when both a and b are both negative. For example,
$\sqrt{-25} \cdot \sqrt{-4} = 5i \cdot 2i = 10i^2 = -10$ but $\sqrt{-25 \cdot -4} = \sqrt{100} = 10$. Since
$10 \neq -10, \sqrt{-25} \cdot \sqrt{-4} \neq \sqrt{-25 \cdot -4}$.

<u>Problem 3</u>
Simplify $\sqrt{-200}$.

$$\sqrt{-200} = \sqrt{-1 \cdot 2 \cdot 2 \cdot 2 \cdot 5 \cdot 5} = \sqrt{-1} \cdot \sqrt{2^2} \cdot \sqrt{2} \cdot \sqrt{5^2} = i \cdot 2 \cdot \sqrt{2} \cdot 5 = 10i\sqrt{2}.$$

<u>Problem 4</u>
Simplify the following expressions.
$$(2 + 3i) + (6 - 2i)$$
$$(2 + 3i) - (6 - 2i)$$
$$(2 + 3i)(6 - 2i)$$

The commutative, associative, and distributive properties are true for complex numbers. Complex expressions can be simplified just as real variable expressions are simplified. Keep in mind, however, that i is not a variable but is rather the imaginary number, so be sure to simplify i^2 to -1.

$$(2 + 3i) + (6 - 2i) = 8 + i$$
$$(2 + 3i) - (6 - 2i) = -4 + 5i$$
$$(2 + 3i)(6 - 2i) = 12 - 4i + 18i - 6i^2 = 12 + 14i + 6 = 18 + 14i$$

<u>Problem 5</u>
Simplify $3i(2 + 4i) - (6 + 2i)^2$.

The commutative, associative, and distributive properties are true for complex numbers. Complex expressions can be simplified just as real, variable expressions are simplified. Keep in mind, however, that i is not a variable but is rather the imaginary number, so be sure to simplify i^2 to -1.

$$3i(2 + 4i) - (6 + 2i)^2$$
$$6i + 12i^2 - (36 + 24i + 4i^2)$$
$$6i + 12i^2 - 36 - 24i - 4i^2$$
$$-18i + 8i^2 - 36$$
$$-18i - 8 - 36$$
$$-44 - 18i$$

<u>Problem 6</u>
Graph these numbers on the complex plane.

$$-4$$
$$2i$$
$$3 - i$$

The complex plane is created by the intersection of a real, horizontal axis and an imaginary, vertical axis. For a complex number written in the form $a + bi$, a represents the displacement along the real axis and b along the imaginary axis. The number -4 is graphed in its appropriate position on the real number line, while $2i$ is graphed on the imaginary axis since its real number component a is 0. The complex number $3 - i$ is represented by a point on the plane which is three units to the right of the origin and one unit down.

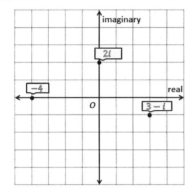

Modulus and conjugate of a complex number

The modulus, or absolute value, of a complex number $z = a + bi$ is the distance from the origin to point z graphed on the complex plane. Since that distance can be represented by the hypotenuse of a right triangle with leg lengths a and b, $|z| = \sqrt{a^2 + b^2}$.
The modulus of a complex number is always a real number.
The modulus of a complex number is always positive.

The modulus of a complex number is always a real number and is always positive. Since a and b represent real numbers, their squares are always positive, real numbers. The sum of two positive, real numbers must also be positive and real, so $a^2 + b^2$ is a positive, real quantity. The square root of a positive, real number is also a positive, real number, so $\sqrt{a^2 + b^2}$ must return a number that is both real and positive.

The conjugate of a complex number $a + bi$ is $a - bi$. The product of a complex number and its conjugate is always real:
$(a + bi)(a - bi) = a^2 - abi + abi - b^2i^2 = a^2 + b^2$. Since a and b are real, and since squares and sums of real numbers are also real, $a^2 + b^2$ is always real.

- 7 -

<u>Example problems</u>
Problem 1: Find the modulus and the conjugate of the complex number $4 + 3i$.

The modulus, or absolute value, of a complex number is the number's distance from the origin when graphed on the complex plane. By graphing $4 + 3i$ on the complex plane, it is easy to see that its distance from the origin is the hypotenuse of a right triangle with leg lengths 4 and 3. Recognize 3-4-5 as a common Pythagorean triple, or evaluate and simply the expression $\sqrt{a^2 + b^2}$, where $a = 4$ and $b = 3$: $\sqrt{4^2 + 3^2} = \sqrt{16 + 9} = \sqrt{25} = 5$. So, the

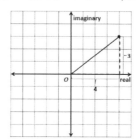

modulus of $4 + 3i$ is 5.
The conjugate of complex number $a + bi$ is defined as $a - bi$, so the conjugate of $4 + 3i$ is $4 - 3i$.

Problem 2: Write an equation which relates complex number z, its conjugate $\bar{z}$, and its modulus$|z|$.

Let $z = a + bi$. By definition, $\bar{z} = a - bi$, and $|z| = \sqrt{a^2 + b^2}$.
Since $z \cdot \bar{z} = (a + bi)(a - bi) = a^2 - abi + abi - b^2i^2 = a^2 + b^2$, and since $|z|^2 = \left(\sqrt{a^2 + b^2}\right)^2 = a^2 + b^2$, we have the relationship $\mathbf{z \cdot \bar{z} = |z|^2}$.

Problem 3: Use the property $z \cdot \bar{z} = |z|^2$, where z is a complex number and $\bar{z}$ and $|z|$are its conjugate and modulus, respectively, to find the modulus of $3 + 4i$.

When $z = 3 + 4i, \bar{z} = 3 - 4i$.
$$|z|^2 = z \cdot \bar{z} = (3 + 4i)(3 - 4i) = 9 - 16i^2 = 25$$
$$|z| = 5$$
The modulus is represents the distance of a complex number from zero on the complex plane and can therefore not be negative. So, the modulus of $3 + 4i$ is 5.

Simplifying the quotient of two complex numbers

<u>Example problems</u>
Problem 1: Simplify $\frac{2-4i}{1+3i}$.

To simplify the quotient of two complex numbers, multiply the numerator and denominator by the complex conjugate of the denominator.
$$\frac{2 - 4i}{1 + 3i} = \frac{2 - 4i}{1 + 3i} \cdot \frac{1 - 3i}{1 - 3i} = \frac{2 - 6i - 4i + 12i^2}{1 - 9i^2} = \frac{2 - 10i - 12}{1 + 9} = \frac{-10 - 10i}{10}$$
$$= -1 - i$$

- 8 -

Problem 2: Simplify $\frac{3-i\sqrt{2}}{3+i\sqrt{2}}$.

To simplify the quotient of two complex numbers, multiply the numerator and denominator by the complex conjugate of the denominator.

$$\frac{3-i\sqrt{2}}{3+i\sqrt{2}} = \frac{3-i\sqrt{2}}{3+i\sqrt{2}} \cdot \frac{3-i\sqrt{2}}{3-i\sqrt{2}} = \frac{9-2i\sqrt{2}+2i^2}{9-2i^2} = \frac{9-2i\sqrt{2}-2}{9+2}$$

$$= \frac{7-2i\sqrt{2}}{11} = \frac{7}{11} - \frac{2\sqrt{2}}{11}i$$

Zero exponent property and negative exponent property

The zero exponent property states $a^0 = 1$ for all $a \neq 0$. The negative exponent property states $a^{-b} = \frac{1}{a^b}$ for all $a \neq 0$.

Consider the series ..., 2, 4, 8, 16, 32, ... Notice that each number is two times the previous number, so the series can be written ..., $2, 2 \cdot 2, 2 \cdot 2 \cdot 2, 2 \cdot 2 \cdot 2 \cdot 2, 2 \cdot 2 \cdot 2 \cdot 2 \cdot 2$, ..., which can be more easily expressed using powers of 2: ..., $2^1, 2^2, 2^3, 2^4, 2^5$, ... The exponent of each number is one more than the exponent of the previous number.

Extend the series a few numbers to the left: ..., $\frac{1}{4}, \frac{1}{2}, 1, 2, 4, 8, 16, 32$, ... Also, apply the pattern of exponents to the series written as powers of two: ..., $2^{-2}, 2^{-1}, 2^0, 2^1, 2^2, 2^3, 2^4, 2^5$, ... Compare the relative positions of newly written terms: $2^0 = 1$; $2^{-1} = \frac{1}{2} = \frac{1}{2^1}$; $2^{-2} = \frac{1}{4} = \frac{1}{2^2}$.

Product of powers property and quotient of powers property

The product of powers property states that when multiplying two monomials with like bases, add together the powers of that base; for example, $x^7 \cdot x^3 = x^{7+3} = x^{10}$ because $(x \cdot x \cdot x \cdot x \cdot x \cdot x \cdot x) \cdot (x \cdot x \cdot x) = x \cdot x \cdot x \cdot x \cdot x \cdot x \cdot x \cdot x \cdot x \cdot x = x^{10}$. The quotient of powers property states that when dividing two monomials with like bases, subtract the powers of that base; for example $\frac{x^7}{x^3} = x^{7-3} = x^4$ because $\frac{x \cdot x \cdot x \cdot x \cdot x \cdot x \cdot x}{x \cdot x \cdot x} = \frac{x}{x} \cdot \frac{x}{x} \cdot \frac{x}{x} \cdot x \cdot x \cdot x \cdot x = 1 \cdot 1 \cdot 1 \cdot x \cdot x \cdot x \cdot x = x^4$.

Power of a product, power of a quotient, and power of a power

The power of a product property states that when multiplying together two monomials with the same power but different bases, multiply the bases and keep the power the same; for example, $x^3 \cdot y^3 = (xy)^3$ because $x^3 \cdot y^3 = x \cdot x \cdot x \cdot y \cdot y \cdot y = x \cdot y \cdot x \cdot y \cdot x \cdot y = (x \cdot y) \cdot (x \cdot y) \cdot (x \cdot y) = (xy)^3$. (Notice the use of the commutative and associate properties of multiplication.) Similarly, the power of a quotient property states that when diving two monomials with the same power but different bases, divide the bases and keep the power the same; for example, $\frac{x^3}{y^3} = \left(\frac{x}{y}\right)^3$ because , $\frac{x^3}{y^3} = \frac{x \cdot x \cdot x}{y \cdot y \cdot y} = \frac{x}{y} \cdot \frac{x}{y} \cdot \frac{x}{y} = \left(\frac{x}{y}\right)^3$. Lastly, the power of a power property states that when raising a monomial to a power, multiply the power of each term in the monomial by the power to which the monomial is raised; for example, $(x^3 y^2)^3 = x^{3\cdot3} y^{2\cdot3} = x^9 y^6$ because $(x^{\wedge}3 \, y^{\wedge}2)^{\wedge}3 = (x \cdot x \cdot x \cdot y \cdot y)(x \cdot x \cdot x \cdot y \cdot y)(x \cdot x \cdot$

$x \cdot y \cdot y) = x \cdot x \cdot x \cdot x \cdot x \cdot x \cdot x \cdot x \cdot x \cdot y \cdot y \cdot y \cdot y \cdot y \cdot y = x^9 y^6$ (Again, notice the use of the commutative and associate properties of multiplication.).

$$\sqrt[n]{x} = x^{\frac{1}{n}}$$

Below is an example illustrating $\sqrt[n]{x} = x^{\frac{1}{n}}$.

$\sqrt{3} = 3^{\frac{1}{2}}$ In this example, $x = 3$ and $n = 2$.

$\left(\sqrt{3}\right)^2 = (3^{\frac{1}{2}})^2$ The inverse operation of taking the square root is raising to the second power. Perform the same operation on both sides of the equation.

$3 = 3^{\frac{1}{2} \cdot 2}$ To raise a power to a power, multiply the powers.

$3 = 3^1$ Simplify. $\frac{1}{2} \cdot 2 = 1$.

$3 = 3$ Simplify. $3^1 = 3$.

Integers and rational numbers closed under certain operations

When two integers are added, subtracted, or multiplied, the resulting sum, difference, or product is also an integer; therefore, the set of integers is closed under these operations. Given that $a, b, c,$ and d are integers and that b and d do not equal zero,

$$\frac{a}{b} + \frac{c}{d} = \frac{ad + bc}{bd} \text{ and } \frac{a}{b} - \frac{c}{d} = \frac{ad - bc}{bd} \text{ and } \frac{a}{b} \cdot \frac{c}{d} = \frac{ac}{bd}$$

$\frac{a}{b}$ and $\frac{c}{d}$ are rational numbers. The products $ad, bc,$ and bd are integers since the product of two integers is always an integer; likewise, since the sum or difference of two integers is always an integer, $ad + bc$ and $ad - bc$ must also be integers. Therefore, $\frac{ad + bc}{bd}, \frac{ad - bc}{bd},$ and $\frac{ac}{bd}$ represent ratios of two integers and are, by definition, rational. So, the set of rational numbers is closed under addition, subtraction, and multiplication.

Example problems

Problem 1
Simplify the expression $\sqrt[6]{9x^4}$.

$(9x^4)^{\frac{1}{6}}$ Rewrite the expression using rational exponents

$(3^2 x^4)^{\frac{1}{6}}$ Substitute 3^2 for 9.

$3^{\frac{1}{3}} x^{\frac{2}{3}}$ Use the power of a power property of exponents.

$3^{\frac{1}{3}} x^{\frac{1}{3}} x^{\frac{1}{3}}$ Use the product of a power property to rewrite $x^{\frac{2}{3}}$ as the product of $x^{\frac{1}{3}}$ and $x^{\frac{1}{3}}$.

$(3xx)^{\frac{1}{3}}$ Use the product of powers property to rewrite the expression

$\sqrt[3]{3x^2}$ Simplify.

Problem 2
Determine if the following statements are true or false. Provide an explanation for the true statement(s) and a counterexample for the false statement(s).
The sum of a rational number and an irrational number is always irrational.
The sum of two irrational numbers is always irrational.

1. It is true that the sum of a rational number and an irrational number is always irrational. Consider for a moment that the statement is false; this would require the existence of some irrational number x that when added to rational number a would produce rational number b: $a + x = b$. Solving the equation for x yields $x = b - a$. The difference of b and a must be rational since the set of rational numbersis closed under subtraction. Since $x = b - a$, x must be a rational number; there is no such irrational number x that when added to a rational number yields a rational number. Therefore, the sum of a rational and an irrational number is always irrational.

2. It is false that the sum of two irrational numbers is always irrational. For example, the sum of irrational numbers $\sqrt{3}$ and $-\sqrt{3}$ is zero, which is rational.

Problem 3
Determine if the following statements are true or false. Provide an explanation for true statements and a counterexample for false statements.
The product of a nonzero rational number and an irrational number is always irrational.
The product of two irrational numbers is always irrational.

1. It is true that the product of a nonzero rational number and an irrational number is always irrational. Consider for a moment that the statement is false; this would require the existence of some irrational number x that when multiplied by rational number a would produce rational number b: $ax = b$. Solving the equation for x yields $x = \frac{b}{a}$; $a \neq 0$. If x is equal to the ratio of two rational numbers, it must also, by definition, be rational. (Note that the ratio of two rational numbers can be rewritten as the ratio of two integers.) So, there is no such irrational number x that when multiplied by a rational number yields a rational number. Therefore, the product of a rational and an irrational number is irrational.

2. It is false that the product of two irrational numbers is always irrational. For example, the product of irrational numbers $\sqrt{3}$ and $-\sqrt{3}$ is -3, which is rational.

Problem 4
Determine if the following statement is always true, sometimes true, or never true: an integer raised to a non-integer power is an integer.

It is sometimes true that an integer raised to a non-integer power is an integer. For example, $4^{\frac{1}{2}} = \sqrt{4} = 2$. However, it is not always true. For example, $3^{\frac{1}{2}} = \sqrt{3}$.

Functions and Equations

Function and relation

When expressing functional relationships, the variables x and y are typically used. These values are often written as the coordinates, (x,y). The x-value is the independent variable and the y-value is the dependent variable. A relation is a set of data in which there is not a unique y-value for each x-value in the data set. This means that there can be two of the same x-values assigned to different y-values. A relation is simply a relationship between the x and y-values in each coordinate but does not apply to the relationship between the values of x and y in the data set. A function is a relation where one quantity depends on the other. For example, the amount of money that you make depends on the number of hours that you work. In a function, each x-value in the data set has one unique y-value because the y-value depends on the x-value.

Determining if an equation or table represents a function

You can determine whether an equation is a function by substituting different values into the equation for x. These values are called input values. All possible input values are referred to as the domain. The result of substituting these values into the equation is called the output, or range. You can display and organize these numbers in a data table. A data table contains the values for x and y, which you can also list as coordinates. In order for a function to exist, the table cannot contain any repeating x-values that correspond with different y-values. If each x-coordinate has a unique y-coordinate, the table contains a function. However, there can be repeating y-values that correspond with different x-values. An example of this is when the function contains an exponent. For example, if $x^2 = y$,$2^2 = 4$, and $(-2)^2 = 4$.

Writing an equation using independent and dependent variables

To write an equation, you must first assign variables to the unknown values in the problem and then translate the words and phrases into expressions containing numbers and symbols. For example, if Ray earns $10 an hour, this can be represented by the expression $10x$, where x is equal to the number of hours that Ray works. The value of x represents the number of hours because it is the independent variable, or the amount that you can choose and can manipulate. To find out how much money, y, he earns in x hours, you would write the equation, $10x = y$. The variable y is the dependent variable because it depends on x and cannot be manipulated. Once you have the equation for the function, you can choose any number of hours to find the corresponding amount that he earns. For example, if you want to know how much he would earn working 36 hours, you would substitute 36 in for x and multiply to find that he would earn $360.

Graphing a function

To graph a function, first create a table of values based on the equation modeled in the problem. Choose x-values (at least 2 for linear functions, more for quadratic) for the table and then substitute them into the equation to find the corresponding y-values. Use each x and y value as a coordinate pair and plot these points on the coordinate grid. Next, connect the points with a line. The graph of a function will show a relationship among the coordinates in that there are no two y-values assigned to each x-value. The vertical line test is used to determine whether a graph contains a function. This states that if you pass a vertical line anywhere along the graph, it will only pass through the graph at one point. If it passes through the graph at more than one point, it is not considered a function.

Using a table to write a function rule

If given a set of data, place the corresponding x and y-values into a table and analyze the relationship between them. Consider what you can do to each x-value to obtain the corresponding y-value. Try adding or subtracting different numbers to and from x and then try multiplying or dividing different numbers to and from x. If none of these operations give you the y-value, try combining the operations. Once you find a rule that works for one pair, make sure to try it with each additional set of ordered pairs in the table. If the same operation or combination of operations satisfies each set of coordinates, then the table contains a function. The rule is then used to write the equation of the function in "$y =$" form.

Graphs of linear and quadratic functions

Linear functions are in the form, $y = x$ and when graphed form a straight line. To graph a function, you need to find at least two points on the line. Choose values for x and substitute them into the equation. Since $y = x$, then $0 = 0, 1 = 1, 2 = 2$, etc. This means that the coordinates $(0, 0)$, $(1, 1)$, and $(2, 2)$ all lie on the line. Quadratic functions are in the form, $y = x^2$ and when graphed form a u-shaped parabola. Every x-value is squared, or multiplied by itself. After multiplying, you will find that the coordinates $(-2, 4)$, $(1, 1)$, and $(2, 4)$ all lie on the parabola. The graphs extend infinitely in both directions and contain an infinite number of points. These graphs are called the parent functions of linear and quadratic equations because they are the most basic in their family of functions; the equations do not contain any coefficients or constants.

Domain, range, continuous data, and discrete data

The domain of a function is the set of all of the possible x-values. These are the values that make the function true. The domain is expressed using inequality symbols and brackets. Often, the domain is all real numbers since these numbers satisfy many functions. The range of a function is the set of all possible y-values, or the result of the values in the domain. To find the range, you substitute the domain values into the equation and express the result within a set of brackets. Linear and quadratic functions contain continuous data. This means the data is represented in an interval and represents a range of data values. This type of data is displayed on the graph with a smooth line and all points on the line are a part of the solution set. Since there are an infinite number of points on a line, we know this represents continuous data. Discrete data values are specific, distinct numbers. This data can be counted and is displayed on the graph as points, or coordinates. The data represented in a scatter plot is an example of discrete data.

Scatter plot

Scatter plots show the relationship between two sets of data. The first step in creating a scatter plot is to collect data. Suppose you are analyzing the relationship between age and hours of sleep. You would collect a representative sample of the population using a list or chart to organize your data. Next, you would arrange the data in a table with the independent variable on the left-hand side and the dependent variable on the right-hand side. To graph your data, look at the range in the values. In this situation, the independent variable, or x-values, and the dependent variable, or y-values, all are positive so you only need to draw and label Quadrant I on the coordinate grid. Look at the data and find the most appropriate intervals to label the axes. Plot the points using (x, y), moving over x units on the horizontal axis and up y units on the vertical axis to see the relationship between the two data sets.

Correlation

A scatter plot is a way to represent the relationship between two data sets. The data can have one of three types of relationships, or correlations: a positive correlation, a negative correlation, or no correlation. A positive correlation is one in which the points increase from left to right. A negative correlation is one in which the points decrease from left to right. A scatter plot with no correlation is one in which the points show no relationship and neither rise nor fall. The correlation can help to determine the line of best fit. The line of best fit is a line drawn to best represent the data values. The line usually falls in the middle of the group of points and contains as many points as possible. When a graph has a positive or negative correlation, a line of regression can be drawn to determine an equation based on the relationship. When a graph has no correlation, a regression line cannot be drawn.

Simplifying polynomial expressions

Polynomials are a group of monomials added or subtracted together. Simplifying polynomials requires combining "like" terms. The "like" terms in a polynomial expression are those that have the same variable raised to the same power. It is often helpful to connect the "like" terms with arrows or lines in order to separate them from the other monomials. Once you have determined the "like" terms, you can re-arrange the polynomial by placing them together. Remember to include the sign that is in front of each term. Once the "like" terms are placed together, you can apply each operation and simplify. When adding and subtracting polynomials, only add and subtract the coefficient, or the number part; the variable and exponent stay the same.

Commutative, associative, and distributive properties

The commutative property states that changing the order of the terms in an equation will not change the outcome. You can remember this because "commute" means to move, or travel. For example, $5 + 4 = 9$ and moving the order of the terms, $4 + 5 = 9$, is also true. The commutative property is also true for multiplication: $5 \times 4 = 20$ and $4 \times 5 = 20$. The associative property states that when adding or multiplying, it doesn't matter how you group the terms, the result will be the same. Remember that simplifying within the parenthesis is the first step in using the order of operations. For example, $(2 + 3) + 4 = 9$ and $2 + (3 + 4) = 9$. This simplifies to $5 + 4 = 9$ and $2 + 7 = 9$. Using multiplication $2(3 \times 4) = 24$ and $(2 \times 3)4 = 24$. This simplifies to $2(12) = 24$ and $6(4) = 24$. You can remember this rule because the numbers are grouped, or "associated", with one another. The distributive property states that you multiply the number on the outside of the parenthesis by each number or value on the inside of the parenthesis. For example, $3(5 + 2) = 3(5) + 3(2)$. You can use arrows to help organize your work. Think of distributing as "giving something out."

Equation notation and function notation

Equations use numbers to show the equality of two expressions and use the variables x and y. Equation notation is written in "$y =$" form. Given an equation, you can find values for x and y by inputting a value for x and solving for y. These values are displayed as ordered pairs in a table of values. The ordered pairs can then be used as coordinates to graph the equation. An equation is a function if there is a unique relationship between x and y in that for every x-value, there is only one unique y-value. This can be determined from the graph using the vertical line test, in which a function exists if a vertical line can pass through the line at only one point. Function notation is written in the "$f(x)$" form. The notation y and $f(x)$ are essentially the same, one just refers to an equation and one refers to a function. Knowing that an equation is a function can give you more information about its graph. Functions use equations to represent relationships between quantities. All functions have equations but not all equations are functions.

Domain and range of a function

The domain of a function is all of the possible x-values. The range of a function is all of the possible y-values. You can determine the domain and range of the function by visually inspecting the graph. First look at the domain, or x-values. Where do the x-values begin, and where do they end? This will establish the set of possible x-values. If the values extend indefinitely in both directions from zero, then the domain is all Real Numbers. Next, look at the range, or y-values, and determine the lowest and highest values for y. If the y-values extend indefinitely, then the range is all Real Numbers. Write your domain and range and include any restrictions.

Forms of linear equations

Linear equations can be written in three different forms, each used for a different purpose. The standard form of linear equations is $Ax + By = C$, where A, B and C are integers and A is a positive number. Any equation can be written in this form. This is helpful in solving and graphing systems of equations, where you must compare two or more equations. You can graph an equation in standard form by finding the intercepts. Determine the x-intercept by substituting zero in for y and vice versa. Next, the slope-intercept form of an equation is $y = mx + b$, where m is equal to the slope and b is equal to the y-intercept. You can graph an equation in this form by first plotting the y-intercept. If b is -2, you know that the y-intercept is equal to $(0, -2)$. From this point you can use the slope to create an additional point. If the slope is 4, or $\frac{4}{1}$, you would rise, or move up 4 units and run, or move over 1 unit from the y-intercept. Finally, the point-slope form of an equation is useful when you know the slope and a point on the line. It is written as $y - y_1 = m(x - x_1)$, where m is equal to the slope and (x_1, y_1) is a point on the line. You can graph an equation in point-slope form by plotting the given point and using the slope to plot additional points on the line.

Slope

The slope is the steepness or slant of a line. The steeper the line is, the larger the slope. It can be found on the graph by calculating the change in the y-values divided by the change in the x-values. The formula for slope is $m = \frac{(y_2 - y_1)}{(x_2 - x_1)}$, where (x_1, y_1) and (x_2, y_2) are any two points from the line. The slope of the line gives you an idea of how the data changes. If the line has a positive slope, you know that the data values steadily increase. If the line has a negative slope, the data values steadily decrease. A horizontal line indicates that there is a slope of 0. This is because the y-values do not change and 0 divided by anything is 0. A vertical line has no slope since the x-values do not change. You cannot divide a number by zero, so we say that this line has no slope. Understanding how to find the slope will allow you to write equations in slope-intercept and point-slope form.

Intercepts

The x-intercept is the point on the graph where the line crosses the x-axis. The y-value along the x-axis at this point is 0. The y-intercept is the point of the graph where the line crosses the y-axis. The x-value along the y-axis at this point is 0. This means that to find the x-intercept, you can substitute 0 in for y and to find the y-intercept, you can substitute 0 in for x into the equation. The standard form of an equation makes it easy to find the intercepts using this rule. Once you find the x and y-intercepts, plot the two points and connect them to form a line. The x-intercepts of the graph are also called the roots of the function. The roots give you the number of solutions that an equation has. Since a linear function forms a line, it only crosses the x-axis at one point and therefore only has one solution.

Changing the slope and y-intercept

The slope is the steepness or slant of a line. If you change the value of the slope, it changes the steepness or slant of the line. A positive slope is one that increases from left to right. For example, a line with a slope of 5 increases very quickly, while a line with a slope of $\frac{2}{3}$ increases very slowly. A negative slope is one that decreases from left to right. For example, a line with a slope of $-\frac{1}{2}$ decreases slower than a line with a slope of -6. The y-intercept is the point that the line crosses the y-axis. Changing the y-intercept only raises or lowers the position of the line on the graph. A positive y-intercept falls above the origin and a negative y-intercept falls below the origin.

Direct and inverse variation

A direct variation is one in which the values for x are directly proportional to the values for y. This is expressed as a line on the graph that either steadily increases or decreases. The equation of a direct variation is written as $y = kx$, where k is called the constant of proportionality because y varies directly with x. An inverse variation is one in which the values for x are inversely proportional to the values for y. The graph of an inverse relationship is expressed as a line that curves inward toward the vertex and approaches the x and y-axes but never actually touches them. The equation of an inverse variation is written as $y = \frac{k}{x}$, because y varies inversely with x. A linear function can be a direct variation if the values are proportional. In this situation, the constant of proportionality is relative to the slope, or rate of change of a linear function.

Translating situations into linear inequalities

Inequalities compare two expressions that are not equal. One expression can be greater than, less than, greater than or equal to, or less than or equal to the other expression. Inequality symbols are used to express these comparisons. To translate a situation into an inequality, you must analyze the words that correspond with these symbols. The terms less than or fewer refer to the symbol <. The terms greater than or more refer to the symbol >. The terms less than or equal to, at most, or no more than, refer to the symbol ≤. Finally, the terms greater than or equal to, at least, and no less than, refer to the symbol ≥. When translating, choose a variable to represent the unknown value and then change the words or phrases into symbols. Recall the terms and expressions used to identify addition (sum, increased by, more, total), subtraction (difference, decreased by, less), multiplication (product, of, times, factor) and division (quotient, out of, ratio). For example, if the sum of 2 and a number is at most 12, then you would write, $2 + b \leq 12$.

Solving linear inequalities

Solving linear inequalities is very similar to solving linear equations. You must isolate the variable on one side of the inequality by using the inverse, or opposite operations. To undo addition, you use subtraction and vice versa. To undo multiplication, you use division and vice versa. The only difference in solving linear inequalities occurs when you multiply or divide by a negative number. When this is the case, you must flip the inequality symbol. This means that less than becomes greater than, greater than becomes less than, etc. Another type of inequality is called a compound inequality. A compound inequality contains two inequalities separated by an "and" or an "or" statement. An "and" statement can also consist of a variable sandwiched in the middle of two inequality symbols. To solve this type of inequality, simply separate it into two inequalities applying the middle terms to each. Then, follow the steps to isolate the variable.

Systems of equations

A system of equations is a set of 2 or more equations with the same variables. You can solve systems using the substitution method, the elimination method, matrices, or by graphing the systems. The solution of a system of equations is the value that both or all of the equations share. When looking at the graph of a system, the solution is the point that is shared by all of the equations. These systems are considered consistent because there is always only one solution. Systems can also be inconsistent (when the lines are parallel and there is no solution) or dependent (when the lines are the same and there is infinitely many solutions). Systems are often used to compare situations that involve cost. For example, suppose you are trying to cut costs on your monthly cell phone bill. Company A charges $30 a month for a data plan plus an additional $0.10 per minute to talk and company B charges $50 a month for a data plan and an additional $0.05 per minute to talk. You can write an equation for each situation and then use systems to find out how many minutes you would have to talk for the cost to be the same. This will allow you to determine which cell plan is the better deal for the average number of minutes that you talk per month.

Solving systems of equations and solving systems of inequalities

Solving systems of inequalities is very similar to solving systems of equations in that you are looking for a solution or a range of solutions that satisfy all of the equations in the system. Since solutions to inequalities are within a certain interval, it is best to solve this type of system by graphing. Follow the same steps to graph an inequality as you would an equation, but in addition, shade the portion of the graph that represents the solution. Recall that when graphing an inequality on the coordinate plane, you replace the inequality symbol with an equal sign and draw a solid line if the points are included (greater than or equal to or less than or equal to) or a dashed line if the points are not included (greater than or less than). Then replace the inequality symbol and shade the portion of the graph that is included in the solution. Choose a point that is not on the line and test it in the inequality to see if it is makes sense. In a system, you repeat this process for all of the equations and the solution is the region in which the graphs overlap. This is unlike solving a system of equations, in which the solution is a single point where the lines intersect.

Quadratic function

A quadratic function is a function in the form $y = ax^2 + bx + c$, where a does not equal 0. While a linear function forms a line, a quadratic function forms a parabola, which is a u-shaped figure that either opens upward or downward. A parabola that opens upward is said to be a positive quadratic function and a parabola that opens downward is said to be a negative quadratic function. The shape of a parabola can differ, depending on the values of a, b, and c. All parabolas contain a vertex, which is the highest possible point, the maximum, or the lowest possible point, the minimum. This is the point where the graph begins moving in the opposite direction. A quadratic function can have zero, one, or two solutions, and therefore, zero, one, or two x-intercepts. Recall that the x-intercepts are referred to as the zeros, or roots, of a function. A quadratic function will have only one y-intercept. Understanding the basic components of a quadratic function can give you an idea of the shape of its graph.

Changing values in a quadratic equation change the position of a parabola

A quadratic function is written in the form $y = ax^2 + bx + c$. Changing the leading coefficient, a, in the equation changes the direction of the parabola. If the value of a is positive, the graph opens upward. The vertex of this parabola is the minimum value of the graph. If the value of a is negative, the graph opens downward. The vertex of this parabola is the maximum value of the graph. The leading coefficient, a, also affects the width of the parabola. The closer a is to 0, the wider the parabola will be. The values of b and c both affect the position of the parabola on the graph. The effect from changing b depends on the sign of a. If a is negative, increasing the value of b moves the parabola to the right and decreasing the value of b moves it to the left. If a is positive, changes to b have the opposite effect. The value of c in the quadratic equation represents the y-intercept and therefore, moves the parabola up and down the y-axis. The larger the c-value, the higher the parabola is on the graph.

Solving quadratic equations

One way to find the solution or solutions of a quadratic equation is to use its graph. The solution(s) of a quadratic equation are the values of x when $y = 0$. On the graph, $y = 0$ is where the parabola crosses the x-axis, or the x-intercepts. This is also referred to as the roots, or zeros of a function. Given a graph, you can locate the x-intercepts to find the solutions. If there are no x-intercepts, the function has no solution. If the parabola crosses the x-axis at one point, there is one solution and if it crosses at two points, there are two solutions. Since the solutions exist where $y = 0$, you can also solve the equation by substituting 0 in for y. Then, try factoring the equation by finding the factors of ac that add up to equal b. You can use the guess and check method, the box method, or grouping. Once you find a pair that works, write them as the product of two binomials and set them equal to zero. Finally, solve for x to find the solutions. The last way to solve a quadratic equation is to use the quadratic formula. The quadratic formula is $x = \frac{-b \pm \sqrt{b^2 - 4ac}}{2a}$. Substitute the values of a, b, and c into the formula and solve for x. Remember that ± refers to two different solutions. Always check your solutions with the original equation to make sure they are valid.

Exponential growth and decay functions

Exponential functions are written in the form $f(x) = Ab^x$, where A and b are positive and b is not equal to 1. Exponential functions have a domain of $0 \leq x < \infty$. When b is greater than 1, the function represents exponential growth; when b is less than 1, it represents exponential decay. A can be thought of as the initial value of the function, since the function is equal to A when x equals 0. In exponential growth, the function's value begins at A and increases without bound, increasing by a factor of b every time x increases by 1. In exponential decay, the function's value begins at A and decreases to approach 0. The value decreases by a factor of b every time x increases by 1. Deposited money earning continuous interest is an example of growth that can be modeled exponentially, while the decay of radioactive isotopes is an example of exponential decay.

Example problems

Problem 1
Suppose that the distance Greg travels in his car is represented by the function, $y = x - 5$, where x is equal to the time that it takes him to get to his destination and y is equal to his total distance in miles. How many miles would Greg travel in 90 minutes? Explain how you can use this function to find information about future data.

> If you know the equation of a function, you can determine any value for x and y. Since x is the independent variable, it is the value that you can manipulate. The dependent variable is y because you cannot manipulate, or change, the result. You can choose any value for x to find the corresponding y-value. For example, if it takes Greg 90 minutes to get to his grandmother's house, you can substitute 90 for x to find the total distance. $90 - 5 = 85$, so Greg traveled 85 miles. Using functions and understanding the relationship between distance and time, Greg can determine when he needs to leave for school, work, trips, etc. in order to effectively schedule himself and arrive at the appropriate time.

Problem 2
Consider the following situation: you drive 12 miles to school and maintain a constant speed until you hit traffic at 7:40 am. Once the traffic clears you resume your original speed until you get to school. Explain what the graph of this function would look like.

First, consider the variables that are involved in this situation. You are comparing the miles that you travel to school and the time that it takes you to get there. On the graph, the line that is formed by this relationship represents the speed that you travel. The graph should contain the correct labels and scales with the independent variable, the time, along the x-axis and the dependent variable, the distance, along the y-axis. If you maintain a constant speed, the graph would show a diagonal line increasing from zero. When you are stopped in traffic at 7:40 am, the distance is no longer increasing, however, the time is. Therefore, you would see the line continuing horizontally for a period of time. When the traffic clears, the line would again increase diagonally to represent the resumed speed. You can use the graph to analyze trends in the data in order to predict future events.

Problem 3
List the steps to find g(-3) if $g(x) = 2x^2 + x - 1$.

Substitute (-3) in for every value of x in the function:
$$g(-3) = 2(-3)^2 + (-3) - 1$$

Use the order of operations to simplify. First, simplify the exponents by squaring (-3):
$$g(-3) = 2(9) - 3 - 1$$

Multiply and divide from left to right:
$$g(-3) = 18 - 4$$

Add and subtract from left to right:

$$g(-3) = 14$$

Problem 4
Explain how to find the solution set of $x - 1 \leq -6$ given a replacement set of $\{-7, -2, 0, 6\}$.

To find the solution set, substitute each of the values in the replacement set in for x and determine whether the result satisfies the inequality. Remember that values less than or equal to -6 are all of the values to the left of -6 on the number line, including -6. Inputting -7 into the inequality results in $-8 \leq -6$. This is a true statement. Inputting -2 results in $-3 \leq -6$. This is a false statement. Inputting 0 results in $-1 \leq -6$, which is a false statement. Finally, inputting 6 results in $5 \leq -6$, which is also a false statement. Therefore, the only value from the replacement set that makes sense and satisfies the inequality is 7. The solution is written in set notation using brackets as $\{7\}$.

Problem 5
Describe how to write an equation given the coordinates:
$(2, 4), (3, 5), (4, 6), (5, 7), and (6, 8)$.

To write an equation given a function's coordinates, you must first place the ordered pairs into a table of values containing a column of x-values and a column of the corresponding y-values. Next, analyze the relationship between each x and y value and identify a pattern. Look at the first pair of numbers and determine what you can do to each x-value to get y-value as a result. The first pair is $(2, 4)$, so you could either add two or multiply by two to get a result of four. Choose one of the operations and apply it to the other ordered pairs in the table. The next pair is $(3, 5)$ and $3 + 2 = 5$, but $3 \times 2 \neq 5$. Once you find an operation that satisfies all of the pairs in the table, you can write an equation. Since adding by two is a consistent pattern, the equation that satisfies these coordinates is $y = x + 2$. Check your equation by substituting the remaining numbers from the table into the equation.

Problem 6
Explain the steps required in solving: $15 = -2x + 3$.

To solve an equation, first combine any "like" terms. "Like" terms are those that contain the same variables held to the same power or constants. Next, use inverse operations to isolate the variable on one side of the equation. Since both sides of an equation must remain equal, perform the same operation to both sides so that it remains balanced. When solving multi-step equations, first undo addition and subtraction followed by multiplication and division. In this equation, since the opposite of addition is subtraction, first subtract 3 from both sides of the equation. This simplifies to $12 = -2x$. Next, the opposite, or inverse, of multiplication is division so divide both sides by -2. This results in $-6 = x$, or $x = -6$. When solving equations, always verify your answer by substituting your solution back in to the original equation.

Problem 7
Explain how to determine the missing value in the following coordinates of a function: $(-2, -3), (-1, -2), (0, -1), (1, 0), (2, \_)$.

First, organize the coordinates into a table of values to display the relationships between x and y. A table represents a linear function if there is a consistent pattern between the x and y-values. You must be able to apply the same operation or combination of operations to each x-value to obtain the corresponding y-value. If there is a consistent pattern, a linear equation can be written. Looking at the ordered pairs, you will see that you can subtract 1 from each x-value to obtain the corresponding y-value. Therefore, the equation can be written as, $y = x - 1$. Thus you can input the last x-value of 2 to find the corresponding y-value: $2 - 1 = 1$, so 1 is the missing value.

Problem 8

Describe the method used to find the slope of a line given the equation: $\frac{1}{2}y + 4 = x$.

Given an equation, you can find the slope by rewriting the equation in slope-intercept form. Slope-intercept form is $y = mx + b$, where m is equal to the slope and b is equal to the y-intercept. To rewrite the equation, use inverse operations to move the terms to the corresponding positions and determine the value of m. In the equation $\frac{1}{2}y + 4 = x$, to isolate y, you have to first undo any addition or subtraction. The opposite of addition is subtraction, so subtract 4 from both sides of the equation. This results in $\frac{1}{2}y = x - 4$. Next, y is multiplied by $\frac{1}{2}$ and to undo multiplication, divide both sides by $\frac{1}{2}$. Dividing by a fraction is the same as multiplying by its reciprocal, so multiply both sides by 2. Remember to use the distributive property to multiply 2 by the entire quantity $(x - 4)$. This results in, $y = 2x - 8$; therefore by the slope-intercept form, m or slope is equal to 2.

Problem 9

Describe two methods to find the x and y-intercepts of a line given the following table of values:

x	y
-2	-7
-1	-6
0	-5
1	-4
2	-3

The x-intercept is the point on the graph where y is equal to 0 and the y-intercept is the point on the graph where x is equal to 0. First, begin by looking at the x-values in the table. If you see an ordered pair where x is zero, then the corresponding y-value is the y-intercept. Since when $x = 0, y = -5$, the y-intercept is -5. There are no y-values that equal 0, so the next step is to write an equation. One method is to look for patterns among the ordered pairs. Looking at each x-value, you can see that subtracting 5 gives you the corresponding y-values, so $y = x - 5$. Substituting 0 in for y gives you $0 = x - 5$, which simplifies to $x = 5$. Therefore, the x-intercept is 5. You can also use the slope formula to calculate the change in y-values over the change in x-values. Here, $m = 1$, so you can then substitute this value and the y-intercept, $b = -5$, into the slope-intercept form of an equation, $y = mx + b$. Additionally, you could use the point-slope form using a point from the table and the slope to write the equation.

Problem 10
List the steps required to graph an equation given the points: $(-2, -4)$ and $(-1, 6)$.

Label the ordered pairs, (x_1, y_1) and (x_2, y_2).
Using the equation, $m = \frac{(y_2 - y_1)}{(x_2 - x_1)}$, substitute the ordered pairs into the formula and simplify:
$$m = \frac{6 - (-4)}{-1 - (-2)}$$
Use the rules for subtracting integers to simplify:
$$m = \frac{6 + 4}{-1 + 2}$$
Use the rules for adding integers to simplify:
$$m = \frac{10}{1}$$
Divide to solve:
m = 10
Plot the points $(-2, -4)$ and $(-1, 6)$ on the coordinate grid.
Use the slope of 10 to rise ten units and run one unit in order to plot additional points on the graph.
Connect the points with a straight line.

Problem 11
Explain how to graph and write the equation of a line in slope-intercept form given the slope of 3 containing the point $(-2, 1)$.

To write an equation in slope-intercept form, use the point-slope form, $y - y_1 = m(x - x_1)$. Substitute the slope of 2 into the formula for m and the point $(-2, 1)$ in for (x_1, y_1). Simplify by combining "like" terms and using the opposite operations to isolate y on one side of the equation. This will give you the equation in slope-intercept form, which is $y = 3x + 7$. To graph an equation given the slope and a point on the line, first plot the point, $(-2, 1)$ along the x and y-axis. Then using the slope, rise three units run one unit to create a second point. Recall that any number is a fraction over 1. Next, use the b-value of 7 from the slope-intercept form to plot the y-intercept. Remember at the y-intercept, x is equal to zero so the y-intercept is $(0, 7)$. Connect these points with a straight line.

Problem 12
Explain how to find the zeros of the function $f(x) = -2x + 5$.

The zeros of a function, also called the roots of the function, are the points where the function is equal to zero. On the graph, the zeros of a function are located at the points where the line crosses the x-axis, or the x-intercepts. Recall that at the x-intercept, $f(x)$ is equal to 0, so to find the roots of a function, calculate the x-intercept by substituting 0 in for $f(x)$. In the function $f(x) = -2x + 5 = 0$, isolate the term containing x and solve. $2x = 5$, or $x = 2.5$, so the root of the function is 2.5. Since there is only one root, the line crosses the x-axis at only one point.

Problem 13
Explain how to find the y-intercept and zeros of $-3x + 2y = 6$.

> To find the y-intercept of an equation written in standard form, find the point where $x = 0$ by substituting 0 in for x, which gives: $0 + 2y = 6$. This is the same as $2y = 6$. Next, the opposite of multiplication is division, so divide by 2. This results in $y = 3$. To find the zeros of a function, you simply find the x-intercept. The x-intercept is the point where $y = 0$, so substitute 0 in for y which gives: $-3x + 0 = 6$. This is the same as $-3x = 6$. Again, using inverse operations, divide by -3 to isolate the variable. This results in $x = -2$. Therefore, the y-intercept of the function is $y = 3$ and the zero of the function is $x = -2$.

Problem 14
Describe the graph of $4x - 2y = 12$.

> To find the attributes of a graph, you need to find the domain, range, x and y-intercepts, and the slope. It is also important to determine the shape of the graph. Since the highest power of x is 1, this is a linear function and will form a straight line on the graph. The equation is written in standard form, so you can easily determine the x and y-intercepts by substituting 0 in for the opposite variable. Plugging 0 in for x gives you $y = -6$ and plugging 0 in for y gives you $x = 3$. Therefore, the y-intercept is -6 and the x-intercept, or zero of the function is 3. To find the slope of the line, you can rewrite the equation in slope-intercept form by solving for y. To solve for y, use inverse operations and subtract $4x$ from both sides and then divide by -2. The slope-intercept form of the equation is $y = 2x - 6$. Since $y = mx + b$, where m is equal to the slope, the slope of the line is 2. This means that from each point on the graph, you rise 2 units and then and run 1 unit. Since the slope is positive, the line increases from left to right. The domain and range for this line is all Real Numbers, as the line extends indefinitely in both directions and has a slope.

Problem 15

List the steps used to write the equation of a line in slope-intercept form given the points $(-2, 6)$ and $(2, -2)$.

Use the slope formula, $m = \frac{(y_2 - y_1)}{(x_2 - x_1)}$ to find the slope of the line.

Substitute the values into the formula:

$$m = \frac{-2 - 6}{2 - (-2)}$$

Simplify using the integer rules:

$$m = -\frac{8}{4}, m = -2$$

Use the slope and one point to write the equation in point-slope form:

$$y - y_1 = m(x - x_1)$$

Substitute the values into the formula:

$$y - 6 = -2(x - (-2))$$

Simplify using integer rules and the distributive property:

$$y - 6 = -2x - 4$$

Rewrite the equation in slope-intercept form, $y = mx + b$, by adding 6 to both sides:

$$y = -2x + 2$$

Problem 16

Explain how to graph $10 > -2x + 4$.

In order to graph the inequality $10 > -2x + 4$, you must first solve for x. The opposite of addition is subtraction, so subtract 4 from both sides. This results in, $6 > -2x$. Next, the opposite of multiplication is division, so divide both sides by -2. Don't forget to flip the inequality symbol since you are dividing by a negative number. This results in $-3 < x$. You can rewrite this as $x > -3$. To graph an inequality, you create a number line and put a circle around the value that is being compared to x. If you are graphing a greater than or less than inequality, as the one shown, the circle remains open. This represents all of the values excluding -3. If the inequality happens to be a greater than or equal to or less than or equal to, you draw a closed circle around the value. This would represent all of the values including the number. Finally, take a look at the values that the solution represents and shade the number line in the appropriate direction. You are graphing all of the values greater than -3 and since this is all of the numbers to the right of -3, shade this region on the number line.

Problem 17

Explain how to determine whether $(-2, 4)$ is a solution of the inequality $y \geq -2x + 3$.

> To determine whether a coordinate is a solution of an inequality, you can either use the inequality or its graph. Using $(-2, 4)$ as (x, y), substitute the values into the inequality to see if it makes a true statement. This results in $4 \geq -2(-2) + 3$. Using the integer rules, simplify the right side of the inequality by multiplying and then adding. The result is $4 \geq 7$, which is a false statement. Therefore, the coordinate is not a solution of the inequality. You can also use the graph of an inequality to see if a coordinate is a part of the solution. The graph of an inequality is shaded over the section of the coordinate grid that is included in the solution. The graph of $y \geq -2x + 3$ includes the solid line $y = -2x + 3$ and is shaded to the right of the line, representing all of the points greater than and including the points on the line. This excludes the point $(-2, 4)$, so it is not a solution of the inequality.

Problem 18

List and define Describe how to solve the systems $x + y = 8$ and $-3x - y = 6$ using the substitution method.

> Solving systems using the substitution method involves solving one equation for a given variable and then substituting that value into the other equation. It does not matter which equation you choose to work with or which variable you isolate, the answer will be the same either way. Using mental math, you may notice that isolating a variable in the first equation requires only one step. If you choose to isolate the y, you would use the inverse operations and subtract x from both sides. This would result in $y = -x + 8$. Now, since you have solved one of the equations for y, you can substitute this value in for y in the other equation; $-3x - (-x + 8) = 6$. To solve for x, simplify using the integer rules. This results in, $-3x + x - 8 = 6$, or $-2x - 8 = 6$. Next, add 8 on both sides and the result is $-2x = 14$. Finally divide by -2 to see that $x = -7$. Remember that the solution to a system of equations is the value of both variables that make sense in all equations. Therefore, you must substitute -7 back into one of the equations to find the value for y: $-3(-7) - y = 6$ simplifies to $y = 15$, so the solution is $(-7, 15)$. Always substitute you answer back into both equations to verify that it is correct.

Problem 19

Explain how to solve the system $x + y = 5$ and $-2x + 2y = 14$ using the elimination method.

The elimination method involves adding or subtracting two linear equations that are written in the same form in order to eliminate, or remove, one of the variables. First, make sure that the equations are in the same form. Here, both equations are written in standard form. Next, look at the two x-values and the two y-values. Adding these values together would not eliminate either variable, so think of a number that you could multiply on one equation that would result in the one variable cancelling the other if the equations are added together. Multiplying the first equation by 2 would result in $2x + 2y = 10$, and since $2x + (-2x)$ 0, the x-variable would be eliminated when adding the equations. Choose a method and multiply the entire equation by that value. Line the equations up vertically and add them together. The sum of the x-values is 0, so you are left with, $4y = 24$. Using the inverse operations to isolate the variable, the result is $y = 6$. Finally, use this y-value and substitute it back into one of the original equations to find the value of x. $x + (6) = 5$ simplifies to $x = -1$, so the solution is $(-1, 6)$. Remember to plug these values back into both equations to verify that your answer is correct.

Problem 20

Compare the shape of the graph of $y = -2x^2$ to its parent function.

The parent function is the most basic function in each category. The parent function of a linear function is $y = x$. Recall that a quadratic function is in the form, $y = ax^2 + bx + c$. The parent function of a quadratic function is $y = x^2$. The graph of the quadratic parent function opens upward and is therefore, a positive function. The vertex of the function is at $(0, 0)$, the x-intercept is at $(0, 0)$, and the y-intercept of the function is also at $(0, 0)$. Unlike its parent function, the graph of $y = -2x^2$ opens downward and is a negative function (due to the negative coefficient on the x.) The width of each graph is also slightly different. The graph of $y = -2x^2$ is thinner than its parent function (due to the coefficient on the x being greater than 1.) However, like its parent function, this function also has a vertex of $(0, 0)$, as well as an x and y-intercept of $(0, 0)$. Understanding the components of a function compared to its parent function can help you to predict how changing the values of a, b, and c will affect the shape of its graph.

<u>Problem 21</u>
Describe how to find the roots of $y = x^2 + 6x - 16$ and explain why these values are important.

The roots of a quadratic equation are the solutions when $ax^2 + bx + c = 0$. To find the roots of a quadratic equation, first replace y with 0. If $0 = x^2 + 6x - 16$, then to find the values of x, you can factor the equation if possible. When factoring a quadratic equation where $a = 1$, find the factors of c that add up to b. That is the factors of -16 that add up to 6. The factors of -16 include, -4 and 4, -8 and 2 and -2 and 8. The factors that add up to equal 6 are -2 and 8. Write these factors as the product of two binomials, $0 = (x - 2)(x + 8)$. You can verify that these are the correct factors by using FOIL to multiply them together. Finally, since these binomials multiply together to equal zero, set them each equal to zero and solve for x. This results in $x - 2 = 0$, which simplifies to $x = 2$ and $x + 8 = 0$, which simplifies to $x = -8$. Therefore, the roots of the equation are 2 and -8. These values are important because they tell you where the graph of the equation crosses the x-axis. The points of intersection are $(2, 0)$ and $(-8, 0)$.

<u>Problem 22</u>
List the steps used in solving $y = 2x^2 + 8x + 4$.

First, substitute 0 in for y in the quadratic equation:
$$0 = 2x^2 + 8x + 4$$
Next, factor the quadratic equation. If $a \neq 1$, list the factors of ac, or 8:
$$(1, 8), (-1, -8), (2, 4), (-2, -4)$$
Look for the factors of ac that add up to b, or 8:
Since the equation cannot be factored, substitute the values of a, b, and c into the quadratic formula, $x = \frac{-b \pm \sqrt{b^2 - 4ac}}{2a}$:
$$x = \frac{-8 \pm \sqrt{8^2 - 4(2)(4)}}{2(2)}$$
Use the order of operations to simplify:
$$x = \frac{-8 \pm \sqrt{32}}{4}$$
Reduce and simplify:
$$x = \frac{-8 \pm 4\sqrt{2}}{4}$$
$$x = 2 \pm \sqrt{2}$$
$$x = 2 + \sqrt{2} \ and \ x = 2 - \sqrt{2}$$
Check both solutions with the original equation to make sure they are valid. Simplify the square roots and round to two decimal places.
$$x = 3.41 \ and \ x = 0.59$$

Problem 23

Explain how to multiply $(2x^4)^2(xy)^4 \cdot 4y^3$ using the laws of exponents.

According the order of operations, the first step in simplifying expressions to is to evaluate within the parenthesis. Moving from left to right, the first set of parenthesis contains a power raised to a power. The rules of exponents state that when a power is raised to a power, you multiply the exponents. Since $4 \times 2 = 8$, $(2x^4)^2$ can be written as $4x^8$. The second set of parenthesis raises a product to a power. The rules of exponents state that you raise every value within the parenthesis to the given power. Therefore, $(xy)^4$ can be written as x^4y^4. Combining these terms with the last term gives you, $4x^8 \cdot x^4y^4 \cdot 4y^3$. In this expression, there are powers with the same base. The rules of exponents state that you add powers with the same base, while multiplying the coefficients. You can group the expression as $(4x^8 \cdot x^4) \cdot (y^4 \cdot 4y^3)$ to organize the values with the same base. Then, using this rule add the exponents. The result is $4x^{12} \cdot 4y^7$, or $16y^{12}y^7$.

Problem 24

Describe how to find the value of y when $x = 8$ if y varies inversely with x and when $y = 24$, $x = 4$.

An inverse variation is a special relationship between two variables in which as one value increases, the other decreases. This relationship is represented by the equation $y = \frac{k}{x}$, where k is the constant of proportionality. The constant of proportionality is a way to express how the variables change. The first step in finding the missing value in the given relationship is to find the value of k. Use the formula and fill in the missing values. $24 = \frac{k}{4}$. Using inverse operations, you know that the opposite of division is multiplication, so multiply 4 on both sides. The result is $k = 96$. Now, using the formula again, you can find the missing value of y if $x = 8$ by substituting the values into the corresponding positions. The result is $y = \frac{96}{8}$, or $y = 12$. Therefore, if y varies inversely with x, then when $x = 8, y = 12$. You can check your result by looking at the relationship between the two x-values and the two y-values. Since they are inversely related, as the x-values double, the y-values are cut in half.

Solving Functions

Extraneous solution

An extraneous solution is the solution of an equation that arises during the process of solving an equation, which is <u>not</u> a solution of the original equation. When solving a rational equation, each side is often multiplied by x or an expression containing x. Since the value of x is unknown, this may mean multiplying by zero, which will make any equation the true statement $0 = 0$. Similarly, when solving a radical expression, each side of the equation is often squared, or raised to some power. This can also change the sign of unknown expressions. For example, the equation $3 = -3$ is false, but squaring each side gives $9 = 9$, which is true.

General form of a complex number

The general form of a complex number is $a + bi$, where a and b are real numbers. The imaginary number i is equal to the square root of -1: $i = \sqrt{-1}$. Therefore the number i itself is a complex number, with $a = 0$ and $b = 1$. Other examples of complex numbers include $-12i$ and $\sqrt{3} + 4i$. Note that all real numbers are also complex numbers: if $b = 0$, then $a + bi = a + 0i = a$, which is a real number.

Graph of a linear system with no solution

If a linear system has no solution, there is no value of x and y that satisfies both equations of the system. Graphically, this means that the lines that represent each equation of the system will never intersect. Lines that never intersect are by definition parallel. Parallel lines have the same slope, so it can often be determined that a system has no solution without graphing or solving algebraically. For example, if the equations of the system are $y = -2x + 3$ and $y = -2x - 5$, the system has no solution. The equations represent distinct parallel lines.

Possible solutions for a system consisting of a linear and a quadratic equation

For a system that consists of a linear equation and a quadratic equation, it is possible to have 0, 1, or 2 solutions. This is different than a linear system, which has 0 solutions, 1 solutions, or infinitely many solutions. When a linear solution has infinitely many solutions, the two equations in the system are equivalent. A line may never intersect a parabola (0 solutions), or may be tangent to the parabola (1 solution), or may intersect the parabola in two points (2 solutions). Since solving a linear/quadratic system leads to a quadratic equation, it is not possible to have more than 2 solutions; that is, no line can intersect a parabola at more than 2 points.

Example problems

Problem 1
Solve $3x - 2 = -5$ by first assuming the solution exists. Explicitly justify each step.

Assume that the solution exists, and that each side of the equation represents the same real number. In this case, that real number is −5, since the right side of the equation is −5. Adding 2 to each side results in two more equal numbers. So, the equation can be transformed as follows:
$3x - 2 = -5$
$3x - 2 + 2 = -5 + 2$
$3x = -3$

The same approach can be taken with the new equation. Since each side of the equation represents the same real number, divide each side by 3:
$$3x = -3$$
$$\frac{3x}{3} = \frac{-3}{3}$$
$$x = -1$$

The solution of the equation is $x = -1$.

Problem 2
Tom says the equation $3x = 5x$ has no solution. Explain his error.

Tom made an error, because the correct (and only) solution is $x = 0$. Tom may have incorrectly thought that 3 times a number can't possibly equal 5 times the same number, or perhaps he divided each side by the variable x. A correct method of solving the equation would be to assume there is a solution, so that each side equals the same real number. Subtract $3x$ from each side, yielding $0 = 2x$, each side of which equals some real number as well, since $3x$ was a real number. Dividing each side by 2 yields $x = 0$, which is the correct solution.

Problem 3
Find the solution of the equation $x^2 = 36$. Justify your solution method.

One method of solution is to assume there is a solution, so that x^2 and 36 each represent the same real number. Subtract 36 from each side, so that $x^2 - 36 = 0$. The expression on the left side can be factored, and the equation rewritten as $(x + 6)(x - 6) = 0$. If a product of two numbers is equal to zero, then one (or the other) of the numbers must be zero. This leads to the two equations $x + 6 = 0$ and $x - 6 = 0$. Assuming these equations have solutions, add (or subtract) 6 from each side to arrive at the two solutions, $x = -6$ or $x = 6$.

Problem 4

Solve $\frac{6}{x} = \frac{9}{10}$. Explain how each step follows from the equality of numbers.

Assume that the solution exists, and that $\frac{6}{x}$ and $\frac{9}{10}$ equal the same real number. Since $\frac{9}{10}$ is positive, and a positive number divided by a positive number is positive, the value of x must be positive. Multiply each side of the equation by x to get $6 = \frac{9x}{10}$, where each side again represents the same real number. Then multiply each side by $\frac{10}{9}$, to arrive at the solution $\frac{60}{9} = x$.

Problem 5

Solve the rational equation $\frac{2}{x} - 2 = x - 1$.

To solve the rational equation, multiply each side of the equation by the LCD, which is x. This will transform the rational equation into a quadratic equation that can be solved by factoring:

$$\frac{2}{x} - 2 = x - 1$$
$$x\left(\frac{2}{x} - 2\right) = x(x - 1)$$
$$2 - 2x = x^2 - x$$
$$x^2 + x - 2 = 0$$
$$(x + 2)(x - 1) = 0$$
$$x = -2, x = 1$$

Both $x = -2$ and $x = 1$ check out in the original equation. The solution is $x = \{-2, 1\}$.

Problem 6

Solve the radical equation $\sqrt{x - 1} + 3 = x$.

To solve the radical equation, isolate the radical $\sqrt{x - 1}$ on one side of the equation. Then square both sides and solve the resulting quadratic equation:

$$\sqrt{x - 1} + 3 = x$$
$$\sqrt{x - 1} = x - 3$$
$$\left(\sqrt{x - 1}\right)^2 = (x - 3)^2$$
$$x - 1 = x^2 - 6x + 9$$
$$x^2 - 7x + 10 = 0$$
$$(x - 5)(x - 2) = 0$$
$$x = 2, x = 5$$

Only $x = 5$ checks out in the original equation; $\sqrt{2 - 1} + 3 \overset{?}{\Leftrightarrow} 2 \xrightarrow{yields} \sqrt{1} + 3 = 4 \neq 2$! The solution, then, is just $x = \{5\}$.

<u>Problem 7</u>
Solve $x + 1 = \sqrt{x + 1}$. Check for extraneous solutions.

To solve the radical equation, square both sides and solve the resulting quadratic equation by factoring:
$$x + 1 = \sqrt{x + 1}$$
$$(x + 1)^2 = \left(\sqrt{x + 1}\right)^2$$
$$x^2 + 2x + 1 = x + 1$$
$$x^2 + x = 0$$
$$x(x + 1) = 0$$
$$x = -1, x = 0$$

To check whether either solution is extraneous, substitute into the original equation:
$$x + 1 = \sqrt{x + 1} \qquad\qquad x + 1 = \sqrt{x + 1}$$
$$-1 + 1 = \sqrt{-1 + 1} \qquad 0 + 1 = \sqrt{0 + 1}$$
$$0 = 0 \qquad\qquad\qquad 0 = 0$$

Both solutions are valid. The solution is $x = \{-1, 0\}$.

<u>Problem 8</u>
Find the solution of the inequality $-4x + 2 \leq -10$.

To solve the inequality, isolate the variable x on one side. When multiplying or dividing by negative numbers, change the inequality symbol from $\leq$ to $\geq$, <u>or vice versa</u>:
$-4x + 2 \leq -10$
$-4x + 2 - 2 \leq -10 - 2$
$-4x \leq -12$
$$\frac{-4x}{-4} \geq \frac{-12}{-4}$$
$$x \geq 3$$
The solution of the inequality is $x \geq 3$. (Note that when $x = 3$, both sides of the inequality equal -10. Also, when $x = 4$, the inequality is $-14 \leq -10$, which is true. Therefore the solution is correct.)

Problem 9
A softball player's average is the number of hits divided by the number of at-bats. Gene currently has 20 hits in 75 at-bats. If he can get 30 more at-bats, how many hits must he get to have an average of 0.300 or better?

Let h represent the number of additional hits Gene gets in the 30 at-bats. His total number of hits will be $20 + h$, and his total number of at-bats will be $75 + 30 = 105$. The quotient of these two expressions represents Gene's average. Write a greater-than-or-equal-to inequality for this situation:
$$\frac{20 + h}{105} \geq 0.300$$
$$20 + h \geq 31.5$$
$$h \geq 11.5$$

Since there is no such thing as half a hit, Gene needs 12 or more hits in the next 30 at-bats to have an average of 0.300 or better.

Problem 10
A cab company charges $8 to enter the cab, and then $.42 per mile. If the ride cost $19.76, how long was the trip, in miles?

Let m represent the number of miles for a ride in the cab. The total cost is the $8 to enter the cab, plus $.42 per mile. If c represents the total cost for a ride of m miles, an equation for the total cost is $c = 8 + 0.42m$. Substitute 19.76 for c in the equation and solve for m: $8 + 0.42m = 19.76$
$0.42m = 11.76$
$$\frac{0.42m}{0.42} = \frac{11.76}{0.42}$$
$$m = 28$$

A ride that cost $19.76 was 28 miles long.

Problem 11

Solve the linear equation $ax + b = c$, where a, b, and c are real numbers. State any restrictions on the values of a, b, and c.

> The equation can be solved the same way as if the parameters a, b, and c were real numbers. Isolate x on one side of the equation:
>
> $$ax + b = c$$
> $$ax = c - b$$
> $$\frac{ax}{a} = \frac{c - b}{a}$$
> $$x = \frac{c - b}{a}$$
>
> The solution is $x = \frac{c-b}{a}$. Since division by zero is undefined, the value of a must be nonzero. However, if the value of a were zero, the original equation would not be a one-variable equation, but would simply read $b = c$.

Problem 12

Rewrite $x^2 + 4x = 2$ in the form $(x - p)^2 = q$.

> To rewrite $x^2 + 4x = 2$ in the form $(x - p)^2 = q$, complete the square. Begin by adding the square of one half the coefficient of x to each side. In this case, the coefficient is 4, so add $(\frac{1}{2} \cdot 4)^2 = 4$ to both sides, and rewrite the trinomial as a squared binomial:
>
> $$x^2 + 4x = 2$$
> $$x^2 + 4x + 4 = 2 + 4$$
> $$x^2 + 4x + 4 = 6$$
> $$(x + 2)^2 = 6$$
>
> This equation is in the form $(x - p)^2 = q$, with $p = -2$ and $q = 6$.

Problem 13

Complete the square in the equation $3x^2 - 5x = 2$.

> To complete the square, first divide by 3 so that the leading coefficient (the coefficient of x^2) is 1. Then add the square of one half the coefficient of x to each side of the equation, and rewrite the trinomial as a squared binomial:
>
> $$3x^2 - 5x = 2$$
> $$x^2 - \frac{5}{3}x = \frac{2}{3}$$
> $$x^2 - \frac{5}{3}x + \left(\frac{5}{6}\right)^2 = 2 + \left(\frac{5}{6}\right)^2$$
> $$x^2 - \frac{5}{3}x + \frac{25}{36} = \frac{72}{36} + \frac{25}{36} = \frac{97}{36}$$
> $$\left(x + \frac{5}{6}\right)^2 = \frac{97}{36}$$

Problem 14

Derive the quadratic formula by completing the square in the general quadratic equation $ax^2 + bx + c = 0$.

To derive the quadratic formula by completing the square, follow the steps below.

Starting at $ax^2 + bx + c = 0$, subtract c from both sides, then divide each term by a:

$$x^2 + \frac{b}{a}x = -\frac{c}{a}$$

Complete the square by adding $\left(\frac{1}{2} \cdot \frac{b}{a}\right)^2 = \frac{b^2}{4a^2}$ to both sides:

$$x^2 + \frac{b}{a}x + \frac{b^2}{4a^2} = \frac{b^2}{4a^2} - \frac{c}{a}$$

Rewrite the trinomial on the left side as a perfect square:

$$\left(x + \frac{b}{2a}\right)^2 = \frac{b^2}{4a^2} - \frac{c}{a}$$

Find the common denominator to subtract on the left; then take the square root of both sides:

$$x + \frac{b}{2a} = \pm\sqrt{\frac{b^2 - 4ac}{4a^2}}$$

Solve for x and simplify:

$$x = \frac{-b \pm \sqrt{b^2 - 4ac}}{2a}$$

Problem 15

Compare the quadratic forms $a(x - m)(x - n) = 0$ and $(x - p)^2 = q$. What are the solutions of each equation?

The quadratic equation $a(x - m)(x - n) = 0$ is in factored form. Since the right side of the equation is zero, the factors make it easy to find the solutions: the two equations $x - m = 0$ and $x - n = 0$ give the solutions $x = m$ and $x = n$. The equation $(x - p)^2 = q$ has the form of a quadratic after completing the square, which means the left side is a squared binomial. Taking the square root of each side and then adding p to each side of the equation gives the solutions $x = p \pm \sqrt{q}$.

Solve $4x^2 = 100$ by inspection.

To solve an equation by inspection means to solve using fairly obvious mental math, without performing calculations on paper or with a calculator. Dividing each side of the equation by 4 gives $x^2 = 25$. The two square roots of 25 are –5 and 5, so the solution of the equation is $x = -5$ or $x = 5$. A check of each solution (by substituting into the original equation) can seem self-evident:

$4x^2 = 100$ $4x^2 = 100$
$4(-5)^2 = 100$ $4(5)^2 = 100$
$4(25) = 100$ $4(25) = 100$
$100 = 100$ $100 = 100$

Problem 17
Write the quadratic formula. Apply it to solve the equation $2x^2 = 5x - 1$.

The quadratic formula is $x = \frac{-b \pm \sqrt{b^2 - 4ac}}{2a}$. It gives the solution of the quadratic equation $ax^2 + bx + c = 0$. The equation $2x^2 = 5x - 1$ can be written in this form as $2x^2 - 5x + 1 = 0$. Substitute into the quadratic formula with $a = 2$, $b = -5$, and $c = 1$:

$$x = \frac{-b \pm \sqrt{b^2 - 4ac}}{2a}$$

$$x = \frac{-(-5) \pm \sqrt{(-5)^2 - 4(2)(1)}}{2(2)}$$

$$x = \frac{5 \pm \sqrt{17}}{4}$$

The solutions of the equation are $x = \frac{5+\sqrt{17}}{4}$ and $x = \frac{5-\sqrt{17}}{4}$.

Problem 18
Bethany claims the solutions of $(x - 2)(x + 3) = -4$ are $x = -3$ and $x = 2$. Explain and correct her error.

Bethany applied the zero product property to an equation that does not equal zero. Although her values of x make the left side of the equation zero, the right side is –4. To correct her error, she should first multiply the binomials, and then write the equation so that the right side is zero:

$(x - 2)(x + 3) = -4$
$x^2 - 2x + 3x - 6 = -4$
$x^2 + x - 6 = -4$
$x^2 + x - 2 = 0$
$(x + 2)(x - 1) = 0$
$x = -2$ or $x = 1$
The solution is $x = \{-2, 1\}$.

<u>Problem 19</u>
Without solving either system, explain why the systems below have the
same solution. Then verify this fact.

$$\begin{cases} x + y = 4 \\ 2x - y = -1 \end{cases} \qquad \begin{cases} x + y = 4 \\ 3x = 3 \end{cases}$$

When comparing the two systems, it is clear that the first equation of each
system is the same. If an equation of one system is a linear combination of
the equations of the other system, then the systems are equivalent and
therefore have the same solution. A linear combination is the sum of two
equations, with either equation possibly multiplied by a real number. Adding
the two equations of the first system results in the equation $3x = 3$. This is
the 2nd equation of the other system, so the systems are equivalent and have
the same solution. The solution is $(x, y) = (1, 3)$ and satisfies both systems.

<u>Problem 20</u>
Show that if (a, b) is the solution to the system on the left below, then it is
also the solution to the system on the right. In the system on the right, one
equation was replaced with the sum of that equation and a multiple of the
first equation.

$$\begin{cases} 3x + 8y = 2 \\ 2x - 5y = -7 \end{cases} \qquad \begin{cases} 3x + 8y = 2 \\ 3x + 8y + k(2x - 5y) = 2 - 7k \end{cases}$$

The solution of the original system is (a, b). Substituting these values for x
and y in the equations gives the following true statements:

$$3a + 8b = 2$$
$$2a - 5b = -7$$

To show that (a, b) is the solution of the system on the right, show that (a, b)
makes both equations true. The first equation $3x + 8y = 2$ is true, because it
is the same equation as the other system and $3a + 8b = 2$. Substituting a and
b for x and y in the second equation gives $3a + 8b + k(2a - 5b) = 2 - 7k$. Using
the two true equations above, substitute 2 for $3a + 8b$ and -7 for $2a - 5b$
gives $2 + k(-7) = 2 - 7k$, which is an identity and true for any value of k.

<u>Problem 21</u>
Solve the system $\begin{cases} x - 4y = 3 \\ 2x + y = -3 \end{cases}$

The first equation of the system is $x - 4y = 3$. This equation can easily be
solved for x, resulting in the equation $x = 4y + 3$. Substitute this expression
for x into the other equation and solve for y:
$2x + y = -3$
$2(4y + 3) + y = -3$
$8y + 6 + y = -3$
$9y = -9$
$y = -1$
Substitute -1 for y in the equation $2x + y = -3$ gives $2x = -2$, and
$x = -1$. The solution of the system is therefore $(-1, -1)$.

<u>Problem 22</u>

Use a graph to approximate the solution of the system $\begin{cases} -x + y = 9 \\ 2x + y = 5 \end{cases}$ to the nearest integer values of x and y.

The solution to a linear system is the intersection of the graphs of the system. The equations can be sketched by using the x- and y- intercepts of each line. For example, for $-x + y = 9$, the x- and y- intercepts are $(-9, 0)$ and $(0, 9)$, respectively. The intercepts for the other equation are determined similarly.

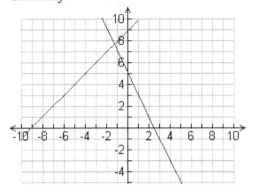

The intersection point is in the second quadrant. To the nearest integer values of x and y, the solution is $(-1, 8)$.

<u>Problem 23</u>

Solve the system $\begin{cases} \dfrac{x}{2} + \dfrac{y}{3} = -1 \\ \dfrac{x}{5} - \dfrac{y}{3} = 1 \end{cases}$. Describe your solution method.

To solve the system, multiply each equation by the least common denominator, or LCD. This will eliminate the fractions, and transform the system into one with integer coefficients.

$$\begin{cases} \left(\dfrac{x}{2} + \dfrac{y}{3} = -1\right) 6 \\ \left(\dfrac{x}{5} - \dfrac{y}{3} = 1\right) 15 \end{cases}$$

$$\begin{cases} 3x + 2y = -6 \\ 3x - 5y = 15 \end{cases}$$

Subtracting the equations results in the equation $7y = -21$, so $y = -3$. Substitute -3 for y into $3x + 2y = -6$ to get $3x = 0$, so $x = 0$. The solution of the system is $(0, -3)$.

Problem 24

At what point or points does the line $y = -x + 2$ intersect a circle with radius 2 and center at the origin?

The equation of a circle centered at the origin with radius r is $x^2 + y^2 = r^2$. For a radius of 2, this becomes $x^2 + y^2 = 4$. Substitute the expression $-x + 2$ for y in the equation of the circle, and solve for x:

$x^2 + y^2 = 4$
$x^2 + (-x + 2)^2 = 4$
$x^2 + x^2 - 4x + 4 = 4$
$2x^2 - 4x = 0$
$2x(x - 2) = 0$
$x = 0, x = 2$

If $x = 0$, then $y = -(0) + 2 = 2$. If $x = 2$, the $y = -(2) + 2 = 0$. The points of intersection, then, are $(0, 2)$ and $(2, 0)$.

Problem 25

Solve the system $\begin{cases} 3x - y = 6 \\ y = 4 - x^2 \end{cases}$, and find any intersection points.

The first equation of the system can be rewritten as $y = 3x - 6$. Substitute the expression $3x - 6$ for y in the quadratic equation:

$y = 4 - x^2$
$3x - 6 = 4 - x^2$
$x^2 + 3x - 10 = 0$
$(x + 5)(x - 2) = 0$
$x = -5, x = 2$

If $x = -5$, then $y = 3(-5) - 6 = -21$. If $x = 2$, then $y = 3(2) - 6 = 0$. The points of intersection are $(-5, -21)$ and $(2, 0)$.

Problem 26

Solve the system $\begin{cases} y = 4 - x^2 \\ y - 3 = 0 \end{cases}$ by graphing.

The equation $y = 4 - x^2$, which can be written as $y = -x^2 + 4$, represents a parabola that opens downward with vertex at $(0, 4)$. The equation $y - 3 = 0$ can be written as $y = 3$, the equation of a horizontal line passing through the point $(0, 3)$. The graph of the equations is shown below.

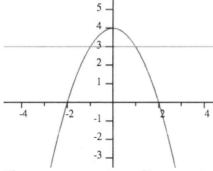

There are two points of intersection of the graphs, $(-1, 3)$ and $(1, 3)$. These are the solutions to the system; both points check out algebraically.

Polynomials and Rational Expressions

Polynomials are closed under multiplication

For a set to have closure under a particular operation, applying the operation to two elements of the set must result in a member of the set. This means that the product of any two polynomials results in another polynomial. This is correct, because every term of a polynomial in x is of the form ax^n, where a is a real number and n is a nonnegative integer. The product of any two such terms would be $ax^m \cdot bx^n = abx^{m+n}$, where ab is a real number and $m + n$ is a nonnegative integer. The last statement relies on the fact that real numbers are closed under multiplication, and nonnegative integers are closed under addition.

Example problems

Problem 1
Subtract the polynomial $3x^2 - 4x + 1$ from the polynomial $-2x^2 - x + 5$.

To subtract polynomials, subtract like terms. Like terms have the same variable part, such as $3x^2$ and $-2x^2$, which are both are x^2 terms. To find the difference of like terms, find the difference of the coefficients, and retain the same variable part. You can use the distributive property to first distribute the subtraction to each term of the polynomial that is being subtracted.
$$(-2x^2 - x + 5) - (3x^2 - 4x + 1) =$$
$$(-2x^2 - x + 5) - 3x^2 + 4x - 1 =$$
$$(-2x^2 - 3x^2) + (-x + 4x) + (5 - 1) =$$
$$-5x^2 + 3x + 4$$

Problem 2
When a polynomial $P(x)$ is divided by $(x + 2)$, the remainder is -4. What is the value of $P(-2)$?

To solve this question, apply the Remainder Theorem for polynomials. The Remainder Theorem states that for a polynomial $P(x)$ and a real number a, the remainder when $P(x)$ is divided by $(x - a)$ is $P(a)$. Since $P(x)$ was divided by the factor $(x + 2)$, let $a = -2$ in the theorem. This means that $P(a) = P(-2)$, and this is equal to the remainder. Since the remainder is -4, it must be that $P(-2) = -4$. Note that it is not required to explicitly know the polynomial $P(x)$ or even its degree to apply the remainder theorem.

Divide the polynomial $x^2 + 2x - 4$ by $(x - 3)$. Verify the Remainder Theorem by evaluating the polynomial at $x = 3$.

Divide the polynomial $x^2 + 2x - 4$ by $(x - 3)$ using synthetic or long division:

$$
\begin{array}{r|rrr}
3 & 1 & 2 & -4 \\
  &   & 3 & 15 \\
\hline
  & 1 & 5 & 11
\end{array}
$$

$$
\begin{array}{r}
x + 5 \\
x - 3\,\overline{)\,x^2 + 2x - 4} \\
\underline{-x^2 + 3x} \\
5x - 4 \\
\underline{-5x + 15} \\
R\ 11
\end{array}
$$

In either case, the remainder is 11. By the Remainder Theorem, for a polynomial $P(x)$ and a real number a, the remainder when $P(x)$ is divided by $(x - a)$ is $P(a)$. In this case, this means the remainder when $x^2 + 2x - 4$ is divided by $(x - 3)$ must be $P(3)$. Verify that $P(3) = 11$ by substituting $x = 3$ into the polynomial:
$(3)^2 + 2(3) - 4 = 9 + 6 - 4 = 11$

Problem 4
Let $P(x)$ be a cubic polynomial function such that $P(2) = P(-1) = P(4) = 0$. If the y-intercept of $P(x)$ is 2, what is the equation for $P(x)$?

By the Remainder Theorem, for a polynomial $P(x)$ and a real number a, the remainder when $P(x)$ is divided by $(x - a)$ is $P(a)$. This means that, since their remainders when divided into $P(x)$ are all zero, $(x - 2)$, $(x + 1)$, and $(x - 4)$ are factors of $P(x)$. Because $P(x)$ is a cubic polynomial function, it must then be of the form $P(x) = a(x - 2)(x + 1)(x - 4)$, where a is some real number. To determine a, use the fact that the y-intercept is 2, which means that $P(0) = 2$:
$P(x) = a(x - 2)(x + 1)(x - 4)$
$P(0) = 2 = a(0 - 2)(0 + 1)(0 - 4) = 8a$
$2 = 8a$
$a = \frac{1}{4}$
The equation for $P(x)$, then, is $P(x) = \frac{1}{4}(x - 2)(x + 1)(x - 4)$.

Problem 5
Find the zeros of $y = 2x^2 + 3x - 5$ by factoring.

The zeros of $y = 2x^2 + 3x - 5$ are the values of x for which $y = 0$. These are also the x-intercepts of the graph of the function. Factor $2x^2 + 3x - 5$ and rewrite the equation as $y = (2x + 5)(x - 1)$. In factored form, the zeros are found by setting each linear factor equal to zero:

$2x - 5 = 0 \qquad\qquad x - 1 = 0$
$\quad 2x = 5 \qquad\qquad\quad x = 1$
$\quad x = \frac{5}{2}$

The zeros of $y = 2x^2 + 3x - 5$ are $x = 1$ and $x = \frac{5}{2}$.

Problem 6
Construct a rough graph of $y = x^3 - x^2 - 12x$.

To construct a rough graph of the function, factor the polynomial $x^3 - x^2 - 12x$ to find the zeros of $y = x^3 - x^2 - 12x$. Because $x^3 - x^2 - 12x = x(x^2 - x - 12) = x(x - 4)(x + 3)$, the function has zeros at $x = 0$, $x = 4$, and $x = -3$. The zeroes are x-intercepts of the graph of the function. The coefficient of the leading term x^3 is positive, and x^3 has an odd degree. Therefore the value of y will approach negative infinity as x goes to negative infinity, and approach positive infinity as x goes to positive infinity. Therefore, the value of y increases from $-\infty$ in the range $x = -\infty$ to $x = -3$ where $y = 0$, continues increasing to a local maximum before decreasing through $y = 0$ at $x = 0$ to some local minimum, and finally increases through $y = 0$ at $x = 4$ to $+\infty$ as x goes to $+\infty$. A rough sketch is shown.

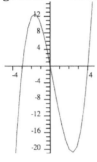

Problem 7
Sketch a cubic function with zeros at $x = -1$ and $x = 3$ that does not pass through the 4th quadrant. Explain your reasoning.

The cubic function has zeros at $x = -1$ and $x = 3$, so these will be x-intercepts of the function. The function does not pass through the 4th quadrant, which must mean that the curve is tangent to the x-axis at $(3, 0)$, and does not pass through the x-axis at this point. For this same reason, the value of y will approach negative infinity as x goes to negative infinity, and approach positive infinity as x goes to positive infinity. A possible sketch is shown.

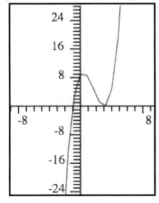

- 43 -

<u>Problem 8</u>
Write the equation for the parabola shown.

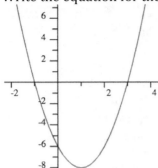

To determine the equation for the parabola, identify the zeros from the graph. The zeros are $x = -1$ and $x = 3$, which means that $(x + 1)$ and $(x - 3)$ are factors of the polynomial that represents the function. Since the parabola is the graph of a quadratic equation, write $y = a(x + 1)(x - 3)$. To determine the value of a, use the fact that the graph passes through the point $(0, -6)$:

$$y = a(x + 1)(x - 3)$$
$$-6 = a(0 + 1)(0 - 3)$$
$$-6 = -3a$$
$$a = 2$$

Therefore, the equation for the parabola is $y = 2(x + 1)(x - 3)$.

<u>Problem 9</u>
Tony has 4 sections of fence that are m feet long, and 4 sections of fence that are n feet long. He encloses two square areas with the fencing, one of side m and one of side n. How much more area can he enclose by making one large square area instead?

Sketch a diagram of what Tony did:

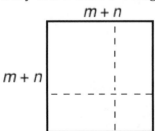

The total area of the enclosures is $m^2 + n^2$. Now sketch a diagram of how Tony could make one large enclosure:

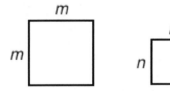

The total area of this enclosure is $(m + n)^2 = m^2 + 2mn + n^2$. Therefore one large fenced area encloses $2mn$ more square feet.

Problem 10

Explain how the expressions m, $\frac{m^2-1}{2}$, and $\frac{m^2+1}{2}$ can be used to generate Pythagorean triples for certain values of m.

A Pythagorean triple is a set of three positive integers that satisfy the Pythagorean Theorem, $a^2 + b^2 = c^2$. For example, the set of numbers $\{3, 4, 5\}$ is a Pythagorean triple since $3^2 + 4^2 = 5^2$. To show how the given expressions can be used, show that the sum of the squares of two of the expressions equals the square of the remaining term:

$$m^2 + \left(\frac{m^2-1}{2}\right)^2 = m^2 + \left(\frac{m^2-1}{2}\right)\left(\frac{m^2-1}{2}\right) = m^2 + \frac{1}{4}(m^4 - 2m^2 + 1)$$

$$= \frac{1}{4}(4m^2 + m^4 - 2m^2 + 1) = \frac{1}{4}(m^4 + 2m^2 + 1)$$

$$= \frac{1}{4}(m^2 + 1)^2 = \left(\frac{m^2+1}{2}\right)^2$$

Clearly, the divisions by 2 require the numerators of those expressions to be even (in order to produce integer results). This occurs for odd m. For $m = 1$, though, one of the terms becomes 0, which is, of course, not allowable. Since negative m produce identical values, for odd m such that $|m| \geq 3$, the expressions generate Pythagorean triples

Problem 11

Show that the sum of the squares of three consecutive integers a, b, and c, is given by the expression $3b^2 + 2$, where b is the middle integer.

Examples of three consecutive integers are 4, 5, and 6, or 21, 22, and 23. If x represents the middle of 3 consecutive integers, then the other two integers are given by the expressions $x + 1$ and $x - 1$. The squares of these expressions are x^2, $(x + 1)^2$, and $(x - 1)^2$. Now show that $x^2 + (x + 1)^2 + (x - 1)^2 = 3x^2 + 2$:

$$x^2 + (x + 1)^2 + (x - 1)^2 =$$
$$x^2 + x^2 + 2x + 1 + x^2 - 2x + 1 =$$
$$3x^2 + 2$$

Problem 12

Expand the expression $(b - 2)^4$ using the Binomial Theorem.

The Binomial Theorem is shown below.
$(x + y)^n = a_0 x^n y^0 + a_1 x^{n-1} y^1 + a_2 x^{n-2} y^2 + \cdots + a_{n-1} x^1 y^{n-1} + a_n x^0 y^n$,
where the coefficients $a_0, a_1, ..., a_n$ are given by the $(n + 1)$th row of Pascal's Triangle. Applying the formula with $x = b$ and $y = -2$ gives: $(b - 2)^4 =$
$a_0 b^4 (-2)^0 + a_1 b^3 (-2)^1 + a_2 b^2 (-2)^2 + a_3 b^1 (-2)^3 + a_4 b^0 (-2)^4 = a_0 b^4 - 2a_1 b^3 + 4a_2 b^2 - 8a_3 b + 16a_4$
The coefficients $a_0, a_1, ..., a_n$ are given by the 5th row of Pascal's Triangle, which is 1, 4, 6, 4, 1. So the expansion becomes
$b^4 - 8b^3 + 24b^2 - 32b + 16$.

<u>Problem 13</u>
Write the 6th row of Pascal's Triangle. Describe what you did.

Pascal's Triangle is a pattern of numbers that give the coefficients of the terms in a binomial expansion. The numbers in row $(n + 1)$ of the triangle represent the coefficients for the terms of the expansion $(x + y)^n$. The first 4 rows of the triangle are shown below:

$$1$$
$$1 \quad 1$$
$$1 \quad 2 \quad 1$$
$$1 \quad 3 \quad 3 \quad 1$$

The pattern continues indefinitely, where each entry is the sum of the two entries diagonally above it. The first and last entries of every row are 1. Therefore, the next row of the triangle will be 1, 4, 6, 4, 1. The 6th row of Pascal's Triangle is 1, (1 + 4), (4 + 6), (6 + 4), (4 + 1), 1 = 1, 5, 10, 10, 5, 1.

<u>Problem 14</u>
What is the coefficient of the x^5 term in the expansion of $(2x - 1)^5$?

The Binomial Theorem gives the expansion of the expression $(x + y)^n$, where x and y are real numbers and n is a positive integer. The theorem can be written as follows:
$$(x + y)^n = a_0 x^n y^0 + a_1 x^{n-1} y^1 + a_2 x^{n-2} y^2 + \cdots + a_{n-1} x^1 y^{n-1} + a_n x^0 y^n,$$
where the coefficients $a_0, a_1, ..., a_n$ are given by the $(n + 1)$th row of Pascal's Triangle. Since n = 5, use the 6th row of the Triangle, which has the values 1, 5, 10, 10, 5, and 1. The x^5 term is the first term; $a_0 = 1$. The x^5 term is therefore $1(2x)^5(-1)^0 = 32x^5$. The coefficient of the x^5 term is 32.

<u>Problem 15</u>
Find the remainder when $2b^2 + 3b + 2$ is divided by $2b + 1$.

The remainder when $2b^2 + 3b + 2$ is divided by $2b + 1$ can be found by long division. To divide polynomials using long division, find the first term of the quotient by dividing $2b^2$ by $2b$, which gives b. Multiply this by the divisor to get $2b^2 + b$, and then subtract this result from the first two terms of the dividend to obtain $2b$. Then bring down the +2 to form $2b + 2$, and continue in this way. The complete division is shown below.

When the degree of the result after a subtraction is less than that of the divisor, the result is the remainder. So, the remainder is 1, and $2b^2 + 3b + 2$ divided by $2b + 1$ is equal to $b + 1 + \frac{1}{2b+1}$.
(Note: synthetic division cannot be used in this case, since the divisor is not a linear factor.)

Problem 16

Rewrite the rational expression $\frac{3x^3+2x^2}{x}$ by inspection.

The rational expression has a monomial for a denominator. This means that when each term of the numerator is divided by the denominator, the result of each division can be found by applying properties of exponents. In particular, the property $\frac{x^n}{x^m} = x^{n-m}$ can be used to rewrite each term as shown:

$$\frac{3x^3 + 2x^2}{x} = \frac{3x^3}{x} + \frac{2x^2}{x} = 3x^2 + 2x$$

The polynomial $3x^2 + 2x$ is equivalent to the original rational expression. Note that the only exception is the value $x = 0$, because the original rational expression is undefined for $x = 0$.

Problem 17

A computer program divides the polynomial $4b^5 + 3b^4 - 7b^2 + 3b - 2$ by the binomial $3b - 2$. The output below shows the coefficients of the terms of the quotient, with the last value equal to the numerator of the remainder.

OUTPUT: 4 7 7 0 3 1

Write the rational expression that represents this result.

The polynomial that represents the dividend is of degree 5, and the divisor is a binomial of degree 1. This means that the first term of the quotient with be a term of degree 4. The numbers 4, 7, 7, 0, and 3 are therefore the coefficients of the terms with variable parts b^4, b^3, b^2, b, and then a constant term of 3. The 0 indicates that there is no b term. The denominator of the remainder is equal to the divisor $3b - 2$. The rational expression that equals $4b^5 + 3b^4 - 7b^2 + 3b - 2$ divided by the binomial $3b - 2$ is $4b^4 + 7b^3 + 7b^2 + 3 + \frac{1}{3b-2}$.

Problem 18

Add the expressions $\frac{1}{x+1} + \frac{x}{x+1}$ and simplify the result.

To add rational expressions, first obtain a common denominator. Then add the numerators, and keep the same denominator. Since the denominator of each expression is $x + 1$, the expressions can be added directly:

$$\frac{1}{x+1} + \frac{x}{x+1} = \frac{1+x}{x+1}$$

The expressions $1 + x$ and $x + 1$ are equivalent. By dividing the numerator and denominator by $x + 1$, the expression can be further simplified:

$$\frac{1+x}{x+1} = \frac{x+1}{x+1} = 1$$

The sum of the rational expressions is equal to 1. This is true for all values of x except $x = -1$, since the original expressions are undefined for $x = -1$.

What is the least common denominator of $\dfrac{3x}{x^2-x-6}$ and $\dfrac{2x}{x^2-6x+9}$?

To determine the least common denominator, or LCD, of two rational expressions, factor the denominators completely. The LCD is equal to the product of the greatest occurring power of each unique factor.
$x^2 - x - 6 = (x - 3)(x + 2)$
$x^2 - 6x + 9 = (x - 3)^2$
The unique factors are $(x + 2)$ and $(x - 3)$. The greatest occurring power of $(x - 3)$ is 2. Therefore the LCD of the two expressions is
$(x + 2)(x - 3)^2$.

Problem 20

Multiply the expressions $\dfrac{1-x}{x^2+2x+1}$ and $\dfrac{5}{x^2-1}$. Simplify the result.

To multiply two rational expressions, multiply the numerators to obtain the new numerator, and multiply the denominators to obtain the new denominator:
$$\frac{1-x}{x^2+2x+1} \cdot \frac{5}{x^2-1} = \frac{5(1-x)}{(x^2+2x+1)(x^2-1)}$$
To simplify the result, factor the numerator and denominator completely. The factor $1 - x$ in the numerator can be rewritten as $-(x - 1)$, and the common factor $(x - 1)$ in the numerator and denominator can be cancelled:
$$\frac{5(1-x)}{(x^2+2x+1)(x^2-1)} = \frac{-5(x-1)}{(x+1)(x+1)(x+1)(x-1)} = \frac{-5}{(x+1)^3}$$
Note that this expression is equivalent to the original product for all x except $x = \pm 1$, since the original expressions are undefined for these values.

Problem 21

If $p(x)$ is a polynomial and $\dfrac{p(x)}{x-3}$ leaves a reminder of -6, what is $p(3)$?

By the Remainder Theorem, for a polynomial $p(x)$ and a real number a, the remainder when $p(x)$ is divided by $(x - a)$ is $p(a)$. In the given equation, $p(x)$ is divided by the binomial $x - 3$, and leaves a reminder of -6. This means that the value of $p(3)$ is -6. Note that the theorem can be applied without needing to know the actual terms of the polynomial $p(x)$.

Problem 22

What are the zeros of the polynomial $(2x - 1)(x^2 - 9)$?

The zeros of the polynomial can be determined by factoring. The expression $x^2 - 9$ is a difference of squares, and factors as $(x - 3)(x + 3)$. The factored form of the full polynomial is therefore $(2x - 1)(x - 3)(x + 3)$. Set each of the linear factors equal to zero and solve for x:

$2x - 1 = 0$	$x - 3 = 0$	$x + 3 = 0$
$2x = 1$	$x = 3$	$x = -3$
$x = \dfrac{1}{2}$		

The zeros of the polynomial are $\dfrac{1}{2}$, 3, and -3.

Prove that the product of two consecutive even or odd integers is equal to 1 less than the square of their mean.

Let n represent the first of two consecutive even or odd integers. Then the following consecutive integer is given by the expression $n + 2$. The mean of the two numbers is $n + 1$, since $\frac{n+n+2}{2} = \frac{2n+2}{2} = n + 1$. One less than the square of this expression is written as $(n + 1)^2 - 1$. Show that this expression is equal to the product of the two consecutive even or odd integers by factoring the expression as a difference of squares:
$(n + 1)^2 - 1 = (n + 1 - 1)(n + 1 + 1) = (n + 0)(n + 2) = n(n + 2)$

Problem 24
What is the constant term in the expansion of $(-2 - 4m)^5$?

The Binomial Theorem gives the expansion of the expression $(x + y)^n$, where x and y are real numbers and n is a positive integer. The theorem can be written as follows:
$(x + y)^n = a_0 x^n y^0 + a_1 x^{n-1} y^1 + a_2 x^{n-2} y^2 + \cdots + a_{n-1} x^1 y^{n-1} + a_n x^0 y^n$,
where the coefficients $a_0, a_1,..., a_n$ are given by the $(n + 1)$th row of Pascal's Triangle. For the expression $(-2 - 4m)^5$, let $x = -2$ and $y = 4m$ in the equation above. The first term, $a_0 x^n y^0$, must represent the constant term in this case, since the variable y is raised to the power of zero. Also, the first term in each row of Pascal's Triangle is one, so a_0 is 1. The constant term is therefore $1(-2)^5 = -32$.

Problem 25
Simplify the rational expression $\frac{x-1}{1-x^2}$.

To simplify a rational expression, factor the numerator and denominator completely. Factors that are the same and appear in the numerator and denominator have a ratio of 1. The denominator, $1 - x^2$, is a difference of squares. It can be factored as $(1 - x)(1 + x)$. The factor $1 - x$ and the numerator $x - 1$ are opposites, and have a ratio of -1. Rewrite the numerator as $-1(1 - x)$. So, the rational expression can be simplified as follows:
$$\frac{x - 1}{1 - x^2} = \frac{-1(1 - x)}{(1 - x)(1 + x)} = \frac{-1}{1 + x}$$
(Note that since the original expression is defined for $x \neq \{-1, 1\}$, the simplified expression has the same restrictions.)

<u>Problem 26</u>
Alison knows that rational expressions are closed under division, assuming a nonzero divisor. She then claims that since all polynomials are rational expressions, polynomials are also closed under division, assuming a nonzero divisor. Explain her error.

> Alison is correct that rational expressions are closed under division, assuming a nonzero divisor. She is also correct in saying that all polynomials are rational expressions, since the polynomial could be written with a denominator of 1, such as $3x^2 + 4 = \frac{3x^2+4}{1}$. However, closure of rational expressions only guarantees that dividing one rational expression by another results in a rational expression. Polynomials are a subset of the rational expressions, but the ratio of two polynomials is only a polynomial if the divisor is a nonzero constant. Since there are divisors of polynomials that do not yield polynomial quotients, polynomials are not closed under division.

<u>Problem 27</u>
Simplify the quotient: $\frac{x-2}{3x} \div \frac{x^2-4}{6x^2}$.

> To simplify the quotient, first rewrite it as a product by taking the reciprocal of the divisor. Then completely factor the numerators and denominators, and simplify by recognizing identical factors in the numerator and the denominator have a ratio of 1:
>
> $$\frac{x-2}{3x} \div \frac{x^2-4}{6x^2} =$$
> $$\frac{x-2}{3x} \cdot \frac{6x^2}{x^2-4} =$$
> $$\frac{x-2}{3x} \cdot \frac{2x(3x)}{(x-2)(x+2)} =$$
> $$\frac{2x}{x+2}$$

Rational expressions are closed under subtraction using closure properties of polynomials

Rational expressions are closed under subtraction if the difference of any two rational expressions results in a rational expression. Consider two rational expressions $\frac{a(x)}{b(x)}$ and $\frac{c(x)}{d(x)}$, where $a(x)$, $b(x)$, $c(x)$, and $d(x)$ are polynomials. Their difference can be written as follows:
$$\frac{a(x)}{b(x)} - \frac{c(x)}{d(x)} = \frac{a(x) \cdot d(x) - b(x) \cdot c(x)}{b(x) \cdot d(x)}$$
Since polynomials are closed under multiplication, the products in the right side of the equation (including the denominator) are all polynomials. Since polynomials are closed under subtraction, the numerator is also a polynomial. So, the expression is a ratio of polynomials and is therefore a rational expression.

Sum of two cubic polynomials

The sum of two cubic polynomials is not necessarily a cubic polynomial. However, it is either a cubic polynomial or a polynomial of lesser degree. The sum of two cubic polynomials of the form $ax^3 + bx^2 + cx + d$, where $a \neq 0$, will have the same form, however it is possible that individual like terms are opposites and have a sum of 0. For example, the sum of $-3x^3 + 2x - 3$ and $3x^3 + 5x^2$ is $5x^2 + 2x - 3$, which is a quadratic polynomial. (Notice that coefficients b, c, and d in the cubic polynomial form are each allowed to equal zero; that is, cubic polynomials can be missing any of the terms with degree less than 3.)

Multiplying a binomial and a trinomial

To multiply a binomial and a trinomial, use the distributive property. Because a binomial has 2 terms and a trinomial has 3 terms, there will be $2 \cdot 3 = 6$ multiplications when multiplying the polynomials. In the example below, each term of the binomial is multiplied by the entire trinomial. Then, that multiplication is distributed to each term of the trinomial. In the final steps, like terms are combined and the answer is expressed in standard form, with terms written in order of descending degree.
$(x + 2)(x^2 - 3x + 9) = x(x^2 - 3x + 9) + 2(x^2 - 3x + 9) =$
$x^3 - 3x^2 + 9x + 2x^2 - 6x + 18 =$
$x^3 - x^2 + 3x + 18$

Remainder Theorem for polynomials

The Remainder Theorem for polynomials states that for a polynomial $P(x)$ and a real number a, the remainder when $P(x)$ is divided by $(x - a)$ is $P(a)$, the value of the polynomial evaluated at $x = a$. If there is no remainder, that is if the remainder equals 0, then $P(a) = 0$ and $(x - a)$ is a factor of the polynomial $P(x)$. For example, if $P(x) = (2x - 3)(3x + 1)$, this can be written as $P(x) = 6\left(x - \frac{3}{2}\right)\left(x + \frac{1}{3}\right)$. Here $P\left(\frac{3}{2}\right) = 0$ and $P\left(\frac{1}{3}\right) = 0$, so that the remainder is zero when $P(x)$ is divided by $\left(x - \frac{3}{2}\right)$ and $\left(x + \frac{1}{3}\right)$; $\left(x - \frac{3}{2}\right)$ and $\left(x + \frac{1}{3}\right)$ are therefore factors of $P(x)$.
On the other hand, the Remainder Theorem also can be used to obtain the remainder when the above $P(x)$ is divided by any binomial, such as $(x - 4)$:
$$Rem\left[\frac{P(x)}{x - 4}\right] = P(4) = (2(4) - 3)(3(4) + 1) = (8 - 3)(12 + 1) = 5 \cdot 13 = 65$$

Polynomial identity

A polynomial identity refers to two polynomials that can be shown equivalent by factoring, multiplying, or simplifying. For any value or values of the variables in the two polynomials, the values of the expressions will be identical. For example, the difference of squares formula $a^2 - b^2 = (a + b)(a - b)$ is a polynomial identity. The left side can be factored to obtain the right side, and/or the right side can be multiplied to obtain the left side. For any real numbers a and b, $a^2 - b^2$ yields the same result as $(a + b)(a - b)$.

Binomial Theorem for expanding the power of a binomial

The Binomial Theorem gives the expansion of the expression $(x + y)^n$, where x and y are real numbers and n is a positive integer. In other words, it gives a way to write each of the terms of the polynomial that results when $(x + y)$ is written as a multiplicative factor n times. The theorem can be written as follows:

$$(x + y)^n = a_0 x^n y^0 + a_1 x^{n-1} y^1 + a_2 x^{n-2} y^2 + \cdots + a_{n-1} x^1 y^{n-1} + a_n x^0 y^n$$

Where the coefficients a_0, a_1,..., a_n, are given by the $(n + 1)$th row of Pascal's Triangle. Pascal's Triangle is shown below up to $n = 4$, and the pattern continues such that each entry is the sum of the two entries diagonally above it.

```
        1
      1   1
    1   2   1
  1   3   3   1
```

Long division for polynomials

Long division for polynomials is similar to long division of integers. For example, when dividing 385 by 12, you first determine how many times 12 goes into 38 (and write 3 as the corresponding digit of the quotient). Then you subtract 36 from 38, giving 2, and the 5 is brought down to form 25, and so on. With polynomial division, the first term written for the quotient is equal to the first term of the dividend divided by the first term of the divisor. For example, if $5x^2 + 10x + 3$ is being divided by $x - 2$, the first term for the quotient is $\frac{5x^2}{x} = 5x$. $5x$ times $x - 2$ is $5x^2 - 10x$, and then $5x^2 - 10x$ is subtracted from $5x^2 + 10x$, yielding $20x$; the 3 is then brought down to form $20x + 3$. This process continues until the remainder is determined.

Polynomials are not closed under division

Polynomials are additions, subtractions and/or multiplication (but not division by variables) of variable expressions containing only non-negative integer exponents. To prove that polynomials are not closed under division, use a counterexample. Assume that polynomials are closed under division. This means the quotient $(x + 1) \div x = \frac{x+1}{x} = 1 + \frac{1}{x} = 1 + x^{-1}$ would have to be a polynomial. This expression, however, is not a polynomial, because the term x^{-1} contains a negative exponent (or would have to be written as the division by x). All terms of a polynomial must be of the form ax^n, where a is a real number and n is a non-negative integer. Although there are *some* quotients of polynomials that are polynomials, closure requires this to be true for *all* polynomials.

Rational, Quadratic, and Exponential Functions

Number of solutions of a quadratic equation and it's graph

Each real solution of an equation represents a place where the graph of the equation crosses the x-axis. A parabolic graph can cross the x-axis in up to two places, just as a quadratic equation can have up to two real solutions. If the equation has two real solutions, the graph crosses the x-axis in the two places with x-coordinates equal to the two solutions. If the equation has one solution, the vertex of the graph lies at the corresponding coordinate on the x-axis. If the equation has no real solutions, the graph lies entirely above or below the x-axis and does not cross it.

Solving a quadratic inequality of the form $ax^2 + bx + c > 0$ or $ax^2 + bx + c < 0$

We can solve a quadratic inequality either by graphing or by algebraic methods. To solve it by graphing, we graph the corresponding equation $y = ax^2 + bx + c$ as a dashed-line parabola. Then, we can shade either the area below the parabola to represent y-values less than $ax^2 + bx + c$, or above the parabola to represent y-values greater than $ax^2 + bx + c$. Whichever portion of the x-axis is within the region below the parabola represents the solution set of the inequality $ax^2 + bx + c > 0$; whichever portion is within the region above the parabola represents the solution set of the inequality $ax^2 + bx + c < 0$. To solve the inequality algebraically, we find the solutions to the equation $ax^2 + bx + c = 0$. The solution set of the inequality is either the set of values between those two solutions, or the set of values "outside of" those two solutions. To find out which set is correct, we choose an x-value from one of those sets and determine if it makes the inequality true. If so, that set is the solution; if not, the other set is the solution.

Conic sections

There are four basic types of conic section: parabolas, hyperbolas, ellipses, and circles. A parabola is created when a plane intersects a cone at an angle parallel to one side of the cone. A hyperbola is created when a plane intersects a cone at an angle steeper than the side of the cone. The plane always intersects both halves of the cone in this case. An ellipse is created when a plane intersects a cone at an angle shallower than the side of the cone. This creates a closed curve. A circle is a special type of ellipse. It is created when the intersecting plane is parallel to the base of the cone.

Changing h, k, and r for a circle in the Cartesian plane

A circle in the Cartesian plane has the equation $(x - h)^2 + (y - k)^2 = r^2$. The constants h and k represent horizontal and vertical translations of the graph. The center of the circle will be k units above and h units to the right of the origin. Increasing h will move it further to the right and increasing k will move it further up; decreasing either of those constants will have the opposite effect, moving the graph down or to the left. The constant r represents the radius of the circle. Increasing r will make the circle larger and decreasing it will make the circle smaller. All three of these constants are independent of each other; changing two of them at once will, for example, move the circle up and to the left, or move it down and make it smaller, just as if those changes had been made separately.

Standard forms of the equations for a circle, ellipse, parabola, and hyperbola

The standard form for a circle is $x^2 + y^2 = a^2$. The constant a represents the radius of the circle.

The standard form for an ellipse is $\frac{x^2}{a^2} + \frac{y^2}{b^2} = 1$. The constants a and b represent the lengths of the axes.

The standard form for a parabola is $y^2 = 4ax$, or $x^2 = 4ay$. The constant a represents the x- or y-coordinate of the focus.

The standard form for a hyperbola is $\frac{x^2}{a^2} - \frac{y^2}{b^2} = 1$. The constants a and b determine the asymptotes of the hyperbola.

Relationship between graphs of an ellipse and a hyperbola

For the graphs of an ellipse and a hyperbola with the equations $\frac{x^2}{a^2} + \frac{y^2}{b^2} = 1$ and $\frac{x^2}{a^2} - \frac{y^2}{b^2} = 1$ respectively, assuming the same values of a and b for both graphs, the constant a represents the length of the semi major axis of both the ellipse and the hyperbola. This means that the hyperbola's closest points to the origin, the points $(a, 0)$ and $(-a, 0)$, are also the ellipse's farthest points from the origin, and the ellipse and hyperbola are tangent to each other at these two points.

The constant b represents the length of the semi minor axis of the ellipse, and also is the vertical distance from the vertices of the hyperbola to its asymptotes. This means that if a rectangle were drawn between the points (a, b), $(-a, b)$, $(a, -b)$, and $(-a, -b)$, the rectangle would be circumscribed about the ellipse, and the asymptotes of the hyperbola would pass through the corners of the rectangle.

Changing the constants in a quadratic equation of the form y = a(x − h)² + k

The constant a affects the width of the parabola; increasing a makes it narrower and decreasing a makes it wider. This means that increasing a will decrease the distance between the x-intercepts of the graph, and vice versa. The constants h and k represent the coordinates of the parabola's vertex. Increasing h will move the entire parabola to the right and decreasing h will move it to the left; increasing k will move it up and decreasing k will move it down. Moving the parabola to the right or left will move the x-intercepts right or left by the same distance. Moving it up or down can decrease or increase the number of x-intercepts by moving the parabola until it no longer intersects the x-axis (or until it does, if it did not before). Only when k equals zero will the parabola have exactly one x-intercept.

Relationship between the functions y = x² and $y = \sqrt{x}$

At first glance, it may seem that these functions are simply inverses of each other. However, the range of the square root function is limited in a way the domain of the square function is not. The square root function can't take on any positive y-values, so the positive x-values of the square function don't have any corresponding points to map to. Graphically, if the function $y = x^2$ were flipped about the line $y = x$, it would be a sideways parabola, which does not pass the vertical line test and so is not a function. The square root function $y = \sqrt{x}$ actually corresponds to just the top half of this sideways parabola. It could be said that $y = \sqrt{x}$ is the inverse of *half* of the function $y = x^2$: the half to the right of the y-axis.

Example problems

Problem 1
Describe how to find the domain and range of a quadratic function of the form
$y = ax^2 + bx + c$.

A quadratic function of the form described always has a domain that includes all real numbers. To find the range of the function, find the vertex of the parabolic graph and determine whether the parabola opens up or down.

To find the vertex, first find the x-coordinate, which always has the value $\frac{-b}{2a}$. Plug this value into the original equation to find the corresponding y-coordinate.

The sign of the x^2-coefficient a determines whether the parabola is concave up or down. If it is positive, the graph is concave up; if it is negative, the graph is concave down.
If the graph is concave up, the range of the function consists of all y-values greater than or equal to the y-coordinate of the vertex; if the graph is concave down, the range of the function consists of all y-values less than or equal to the y-coordinate of the vertex.
For example, if the vertex is at $(3, 7)$ and the graph is concave down, the range of the function is the set of all y-values less than or equal to 7.

Problem 2
The quadratic equation $4x^2 + bx + 9 = 0$ has only one solution. Find the solution.

For a quadratic equation to have only one solution, its discriminant ($b^2 - 4ac$) must equal zero. In this case, we are given the values of a and c, so we can set $b^2 - 4ac$ equal to zero and solve for b:
$$b^2 - 4ac = 0$$
$$b^2 - 4(4)(9) = 0$$
$$b^2 - 144 = 0$$
$$b^2 = 144$$
$$b = 12$$

Then we can use the quadratic formula to find the solution of the equation. Since we already know that the discriminant equals zero, the equation $x = \frac{-b \pm \sqrt{b^2 - 4ac}}{2a}$ reduces to simply $x = \frac{-b}{2a}$. Substituting 12 for b and 4 for a gives us $x = \frac{-12}{8} = \frac{-3}{2}$.

<u>Problem 3</u>

The quadratic equation $y = ax^2 + 2x - 8$ has -2 as one of its roots. Find the other root.

Based on the root we know, we can determine the missing coefficient a in the quadratic equation. We plug in -2 for x and 0 for y, and solve for a:
$$0 = a(-2)^2 + 2(-2) - 8$$
$$0 = 4a - 4 - 8$$
$$0 = 4a - 12$$
$$4a = 12$$
$$a = 3$$

Then we can find the other root by using the quadratic equation or by factoring. Factoring is easier since we already know one root: the factors are either $(3x + 2)(x + k)$ or $(3x + k)(x + 2)$. Since one root is x=-2, the other root must be $(3x+k)=0$. Trial and error tells us that k = -4, thus $\frac{4}{3}$ is the other root of the equation. We can check this by plugging it in as we did -2 above.

<u>Problem 4</u>

Find the x-coordinate of the vertex for a quadratic equation with the following values:

X	-1	0	1	2	3	4	5
Y	13	5	1	1	5	13	25

One way to find the approximate location of the vertex is by graphing the points in the table, sketching the parabola, and attempting to eyeball the vertex. Another way to find the vertex would be to find the equation of the parabola based on the points in the table, and then convert the equation to vertex form. However, analyzing the values in the table can tell us where the x-coordinate of the vertex is without needing to find the equation or graph it. The y-values are the same for x-values 1 and 2 (as well as for 0 and 3, and for -1 and 4), so the graph of the parabola is symmetric about the line x = 1.5. The vertex must lie on this line of symmetry, so the vertex has x-coordinate 1.5.

Problem 5
Find a quadratic equation whose real roots are x = 2 and x = -1.

One way to find the roots of a quadratic equation is to factor the equation
and use the zero product property, setting each factor of the equation equal
to zero to find the corresponding root. We can use this technique in reverse
to find an equation given its roots. Each root corresponds to a linear
equation which in turn corresponds to a factor of the quadratic equation.

For example, the root $x = 2$ corresponds to the equation x – 2 = 0, and the
root x = -1 corresponds to the equation x + 1 = 0. These two equations
correspond to the factors $(x – 2)$ and $(x + 1)$, from which we can derive the
equation $(x – 2)(x + 1) = 0$, or $x^2 – x – 2 = 0$.

(Any integer multiple of this entire equation will also yield the same roots,
as the integer will simply cancel out when the equation is factored. For
example, $2x^2 – 2x – 4 = 0$ factors as $2(x – 2)(x + 1) = 0$.)

Problem 6
A parabolic graph is concave down, has a y-intercept of -5, and has no x-intercepts. What
can be determined about the equation of the graph?

The equation of a parabola is a quadratic, written in standard form as
$y = ax^2 + bx + c$. Since the graph in this case is concave down, the x^2-
coordinate a must be negative, though we do not know exactly what it is.
We also know that the constant term, c, is equal to the y-intercept, in this
case -5 (We can confirm this algebraically: no matter what a and b are,
plugging the coordinates (0, -5) into the equation gives us -5 = c.).

Finally, the lack of x-intercepts tells us that the equation has no real roots, so
its discriminant, $b^2 – 4ac$, must be negative. Plugging in -5 for c means that
the expression $b^2 + 20a$ is negative. We already know that b^2 must be
positive (because it is the square of a real number), so now we also know
that $-20a$ must be greater than b^2. This puts a limit on the possible values of
a and b, even though we still do not know either of them exactly.

A parabolic graph intersects the x-axis at 1 and 3 and the y-axis at -6. What can be determined about the equation of the graph?

We can determine the entire equation of the graph from these three points. First of all, we know that the solutions of the equation are described by the quadratic formula: $x = \frac{-b \pm \sqrt{b^2 - 4ac}}{2a}$. We also know that c is equal to the y-intercept, which is -6, and we know that the vertex of the equation is midway between the x-intercepts, and its x-coordinate is $\frac{-b}{2a}$. So $\frac{-b}{2a} = 2$, meaning that b = -4a.

Substituting -4a for b and -6 for c in the quadratic formula gives us $x = \frac{4a \pm \sqrt{16a^2 + 24a}}{2a}$, which reduces to x = $2 \pm \frac{\sqrt{4a^2 + 6a}}{a}$. We know that the roots of this equation are 1 and 3, which equal 2 ± 1, so $\frac{\sqrt{4a^2 + 6a}}{a}$ must equal 1 or -1. Solving for a, we find a = -2. This means that b = 8, so the equation of the graph is y = -2x² + 8x -6.

Problem 8
The graph of the equation y = x² + 5x – 6 is translated twelve units upward. What are the x-intercepts of the new graph?

Translating a graph upward simply adds the corresponding number to the constant term of the equation. Moving this graph upward twelve units means we add 12 to the constant term -6, so it becomes 6.

Now we must find the roots of the new equation y = x² + 5x + 6. We can do this through the quadratic equation or by factoring. As it happens, this equation factors handily: (x + 2)(x +3) thus the roots of the equation are -2 and -3.

(Notice that these are unrelated to the roots of the original equation, which are 1 and -6.)

Problem 9
The graph of the equation y = x² + 2x – 8 is translated three units to the left. What are the x-intercepts of the new graph?

There is no simple algebraic transformation representing a horizontal shift of a parabolic graph. We could represent it by substituting (x + 3) for x in the original equation (yielding y = (x+3)² + 2(x+3) – 8 or y = x² + 8x +7) and then simplifying. However, this isn't actually necessary, since all we need to find are the x-intercepts. The x-intercepts of the new graph will simply be the x-intercepts of the old graph shifted three units to the left. Finding the roots of the original equation is simple: the equation factors as (x – 2)(x + 4), so the x-intercepts are at 2 and -4. Therefore, the x-intercepts of the shifted graph will be at (2 – 3) and (-4 – 3), or -1 and -7.

Problem 10

A swimming pool is 11 feet longer than it is wide. The area of the pool is 276 square feet. What are the dimensions of the pool?

> If the width of the pool is x feet, the length is $x + 11$ and the area is therefore $x(x + 11) = x^2 + 11x$ square feet. We therefore have the quadratic equation $x^2 + 11x = 276$, or $x^2 + 11x - 276 = 0$.
> Solving this equation gives us two possible values for x: 12 and -23. It does not make sense for the width of the pool to be -23 feet, so it must be 12 feet. Therefore, the length is $12 + 11 = 23$ feet. Checking this answer, we find that indeed, 12 times 23 is 276 square feet.

Problem 11

Find the vertex of the parabola whose equation is $y = x^2 + 2x - 15$ by translating the equation into the form $y = a(x - h)^2 + k$.

> The coefficient of x^2 in the original equation equals 1, so that is the value of a in the new equation. The remaining constants are then found by completing the square. The value of h is found by taking the opposite of half of the x-coefficient, so $h = -1$. $1(x + 1)^2$ expands to $x^2 + 2x + 1$, and we need to find the value of k to add to this expression to make it equal $x^2 + 2x - 15$; that value is therefore -16. So the final form of the equation is $y = (x + 1)^2 - 16$. The coordinates of the vertex are (h, k), so the vertex is at (-1, 16).

Problem 12

One square picture frame has an area of 31 square inches less than twice the area of another square frame. If the second frame has an area of x square inches, write an expression for the side length of the first frame. Then find the side lengths of the two frames given that the second is 3 inches shorter than the first.

> The first frame's area is 31 less than twice x, or $2x - 31$. Its side length is therefore $\sqrt{2x - 31}$.
>
> The side length of the second frame is $\sqrt{x}$, so an equation relating the two side lengths is $\sqrt{x} + 3 = \sqrt{2x - 31}$.
>
> Since one side of the equation is a radical, we can start by squaring both sides: $x + 6\sqrt{x} + 9 = 2x - 31$.
>
> Then we need to isolate the other radical so we can square both sides again. Subtracting both x and 9 from both sides leaves $6\sqrt{x} = x - 40$; and squaring leaves $36x = x^2 - 80x + 1600$.
>
> Finally, we subtract $36x$ from both sides, giving us $x^2 - 116x + 1600 = 0$, and then solve for x: $x = 16$ or $x = 100$. So the second picture frame is either 4 × 4 inches (making the first frame 1 × 1) or 10 × 10 inches (making the first frame 13 × 13). Since we were told that the second frame is smaller than the first, the second answer is correct.

<u>Problem 13</u>
Find the inverse of the function
$$y = \frac{1}{2}\sqrt{2x + 6} - 1.$$

To find the inverse of a function, we switch the independent and dependent variables and then solve for y. In this case, we start with $x = \frac{1}{2}\sqrt{2y + 6} - 1$, add 1 to both sides, and multiply by 2, yielding $2x + 2 = \sqrt{2y + 6}$.

Now that we have isolated the square root, we can square both sides, giving us $(2x + 2)^2 = 2y + 6$. Expanding the left side gives us $4x^2 + 8x + 4 = 2y + 6$, and then we can isolate y by subtracting 6 from both sides and dividing through by 2. This gives us $y = 2x^2 + 4x - 1$.

Vertical asymptotes of a rational function

The vertical asymptotes of a rational function occur wherever the function is undefined, which is wherever the denominator of the function equals zero and the numerator does not equal zero. To find the vertical asymptotes, we simply find the zeros of the denominator, and eliminate any that are also zeros of the numerator (we can perform this check easily by simply plugging each one into the numerator to see if it causes the numerator to equal zero.) A rational function can therefore have as many vertical asymptotes as the degree of its denominator, but may have fewer.

Horizontal or oblique asymptotes of a rational function

Horizontal or slant asymptotes are the lines that the function may approach as its x-values approach infinity. A rational function can have at most one horizontal or oblique asymptote.

If the degree of the numerator is less than the degree of the denominator, the function has a horizontal asymptote at $y = 0$. If the degree of the numerator equals the degree of the denominator, the function has a horizontal asymptote at $y = c$, where c is the quotient of the highest-degree terms of the numerator and denominator (For example, if the leading term of the numerator is $5x^3$ and the leading term of the denominator is $2x^3$, the asymptote is at $y = \frac{5}{2}$.)

If the degree of the numerator is one greater than the degree of the denominator, then long division must be performed to simplify the entire fraction, and the resulting linear equation is the equation of the slant asymptote.

If the degree of the numerator exceeds the degree of the denominator by more than one, there is no horizontal or slant asymptote.

Example problems

Problem 1
State the domain and range of the function $y = \sqrt{x-3} + 1$

> The domain of a basic square root function is the set of all real numbers greater than or equal to zero. That is because taking the square root of a negative number is not permitted. However, in this function we can see that values of x between 0 and 3 will also result in taking the square root of a negative number, and thus those values must also not be part of the domain. The function's domain is therefore the set of all real numbers greater than or equal to 3.
>
> Since square roots must always be positive, the range of a basic square root function is also the set of all real numbers greater than or equal to zero. In this case, however, the output values of the square root function will all have 1 added to them, so the final value of the function will never be less than 1. The function's range is therefore the set of all real numbers greater than or equal to 1.

Problem 2
Solve the equation $2\sqrt{x^2-5} + 3 = 7$ for x.

> First it is necessary to isolate the square root sign on one side of the equation. Subtracting 3 from both sides and then dividing by 2 gives us $\sqrt{x^2-5} = 2$.
> Squaring both sides is the next step: $x^2 - 5 = 4$.
> Next, adding 5 to both sides yields $x^2 = 9$. This means that x can equal 3 or -3. However, squaring both sides of an equation can introduce extraneous solutions, so each of these solutions needs to be checked in the original equation. In this case, however, both solutions do check out, as they both yield $2\sqrt{9-5} + 3 = 7$.

Problem 3
If y varies directly with x and inversely with $z - x$, for what values of x and z does y have a nonzero value? Does this answer change if y varies directly with $z - x$ and inversely with x?

> If y varies directly with x and inversely with $z - x$, the equation that expresses this variation is $= \frac{kx}{z-x}$, where k is a nonzero constant. This equation will be undefined whenever the denominator of the fraction equals zero (hence whenever $z = x$), and will equal zero whenever the numerator equals zero (hence whenever $x = 0$). At all other times, y will have a nonzero value.
> If y varies directly with $z - x$ and inversely with x, the equation expresses this variation is $= \frac{k(z-x)}{x}$. This equation will be undefined whenever $x = 0$ and will equal zero whenever $z = x$; in other words, it will be undefined at all the points where the previous function equaled zero, and will equal zero at all the points where the previous function was undefined. At all other points, y will have a nonzero value, just as with the previous equation.

Problem 4

Find the asymptotes of the function $\frac{2x^2-2}{x^2+3x-4}$.

Vertical asymptotes occur wherever the denominator, but not the numerator, equals zero. The zeros of the denominator are -4 and 1; the zeros of the numerator are -1 and 1. Therefore, there is a vertical asymptote at x = -4, but not at x = 1 (Simplifying the fraction makes it clear why: the factor (x – 1) simply cancels out.)

The numerator and denominator have the same degree. This means that to find the horizontal asymptote, we find the quotient of the leading terms of the numerator and denominator. $\frac{2x^2}{x^2}$ equals 2, so the function has a horizontal asymptote at y = 2.

Problem 5

The high school science club raised $240 from its members to pay the cost of a chartered bus for a field trip, with each member contributing an equal share. When four members of the club were unable to go on the trip, their money was refunded and each other member had to contribute an extra $2 to cover the bus cost. How many members does the club have?

If we let x equal the number of members, then we know that each member originally paid $\frac{240}{x}$ dollars. We also know that the same cost of $240 was covered by x - 4 members each paying $\frac{240}{x}$ + 2 dollars. So we can write the equation $(x - 4)\left(\frac{240}{x} + 2\right) = 240$ and solve for x.

First, multiplying the terms out gives us $240 + 2x - \frac{960}{x} - 8 = 240$, which simplifies to $2x - \frac{960}{x} - 8 = 0$. If we isolate the fraction on one side $(2x - 8 = \frac{960}{x})$, then we can multiply both sides by x to clear fractions: x(2x – 8) = 960. From there we get the quadratic 2x² – 8x – 960 = 0, which we can solve to get x = -20 and x = 24. 24 is therefore the number of students in the club.

Domain and range

If we think of a function as a procedure that takes a given input and produces a given output, the domain of the function is the set of all permissible inputs and the range is the set of all possible outputs. In other words, any value that we could "plug in" to the function and get a meaningful answer is in the domain of the function, and the answer we would get if we plugged in that value would be in the range of the function. When we plot a function on the xy-coordinate plane, the domain is the set of all x-values covered by the function, and the range is the set of all the y-values.

Scatter plot

Any collection of data points can be displayed as a scatter plot simply by graphing each of the points on a coordinate grid. The resulting graph will be a set of unconnected points rather than a line or curve. However, a line or curve can be found that fits the points approximately, if not exactly. The line or curve of "best fit" can then be used to predict other data points; we simply assume that these data points will lie directly on the line or curve, and use the equation of the line or curve to predict the y-value that will result from each x-value.

Graphs of functions

The graph of a linear function is a straight line.

The graph of a quadratic function is a parabola.

The graph of an exponential function increases more and more rapidly as it moves from left to right, and has a horizontal asymptote at $y = 0$.

A logarithmic function is the inverse of an exponential function. Its graph has a vertical asymptote at $x = 0$, and increases less rapidly as it moves from left to right.

The graph of an absolute value function is like a linear function, but with the negative portion of the graph reflected back across the x-axis.

The graph of a square root function is the upper half of a parabola lying on its side.

The graph of a rational function consists of two branches, one in the first quadrant and one in the third quadrant. Each branch decreases from left to right and has asymptotes at $x = 0$ and $y = 0$.

Changing constants in equations

Linear equations
Changing the constants m and b in a linear equation of the form $y = mx + b$ affects the graph of the function. The constant m represents the slope of the graph. If m is positive, the graph slopes upward from left to right; if m is negative, the graph slopes downward. The greater the absolute value of m, the steeper the slope of the graph. The constant b represents the y-intercept of the graph, but it also represents how far and in what direction the graph has been shifted vertically compared to the base function $y = mx$. Increasing b shifts the graph upward and decreasing b shifts it downward, while the slope of the graph remains the same.

Quadratic equations
Changing the constants a and c in a quadratic equation of the form $y = ax^2 + bx + c$ affects the graph of the function. The x^2-coefficient a determines the width of the parabola described by the equation. A higher value of a means that the parabola slopes upward more steeply, and is therefore narrower. A lower value results in a wider, shallower parabola. Furthermore, a positive value of a means that the parabola is concave up, and a negative value means it is concave down. The constant term c represents a vertical shift of the parabola. Increasing the value of c shifts the parabola upward, and decreasing c shifts it

- 63 -

downward. If c = 0, the parabola passes through the origin (though its vertex is not necessarily at the origin).

<u>Exponential equations</u>
Changing the constant a in an exponential equation of the form $y = a^x$ affects the graph of the function. The orientation of an exponential function graph depends on the magnitude and sign of the base a. If a is positive, the graph lies above the x-axis; if a is negative, the graph lies below the x-axis. If the absolute value of a is greater than 1, the graph approaches the x-axis as it moves to the left and approaches infinity as it moves to the right; if the absolute value of a is less than 1, the graph approaches the x-axis as it moves to the right and approaches infinity as it moves to the left; and if the absolute value of a equals 1, the graph is simply a horizontal line. Furthermore, the graph slopes more steeply upward or downward the farther a is from 1.

Graph of a function and graph of its inverse

The inverse of a function is the same as the original function, only with the independent and dependent variables switched. In other words, the inverse is what results if we take the original function and replace the x's with y's and the y's with x's. Hence, the graph of the inverse function looks the same as the graph of the original function would look if the x-axis and y-axis were exchanged. To swap the positive x-axis with the positive y-axis and the negative x-axis with the negative y-axis, it is necessary to flip the entire coordinate plane about the line $y = x$. Therefore, the graph of the inverse function is simply the graph of the original function flipped about the line $y = x$.

Consistent, inconsistent, and dependent systems of equations

A consistent system of equations has exactly one solution; that is, there is exactly one ordered pair that is a solution to both equations. The graphs of the two equations are lines that intersect at exactly one point.

An inconsistent system has no solutions. The graphs of the two equations are parallel lines.

A dependent system has infinitely many solutions; that is, every ordered pair that is a solution to one equation is a solution to the other equation as well. The graphs of the two equations are both graphs of the same line.

Substitution and elimination for solving linear systems

To solve a linear system by substitution, we rearrange one of the equations to isolate one variable. This tells us what expression to substitute for that variable in the other equation. For example, given the system:

$$x + 3y = 5$$
$$2x - 4y = 3$$

We can rewrite the first equation as $x = 5 - 3y$. Then we can rewrite the second equation as $2(5 - 3y) - 4y = 3$, and solve for y.

To solve a system by elimination, we add multiples of the two equations together in such a way that one variable drops out; then we solve for the remaining variable.

For example, to solve the system given above, we could multiply the first equation by -2, giving us:

$$-2x - 6y = -10$$
$$2x - 4y = 3$$

Adding the two equations together yields 0x – 10y = -7, or simply -10y = -7, which we can then solve for y.

Relationship between the functions y = aˣ and y = logₐ x

The functions $y = a^x$ and $y = \log_a x$ are inverses of each other; that is, for any two numbers p and q, if $p = a^q$ then $q = \log_a p$. Consequently, applying both functions in succession gives us the original input back again; that is, $\log_a(a^x) = x$, and $a^{\log_a x} = x$.

Since the two functions are inverses, their graphs are identical to each other, but flipped about the line y = x. Where the exponential graph has a horizontal asymptote, the logarithmic graph has a vertical asymptote; where the exponential graph slopes more steeply as it moves to the right (or left), the logarithmic graph slopes less steeply.

Terms in the exponential growth formula x(t) = x₀ · eᵏᵗ

$x(t)$ represents the value of the dependent variable x as a function of time (Note that x is the dependent variable here, although we usually see it as the independent variable.) x_0 represents the value of x at time t = 0, which is whatever time we begin measuring. t is the amount of time that has passed since t = 0, and k is the constant of exponential growth. The specific value of k depends on the specific situation being modeled, and a negative value of k indicates that exponential decay, rather than growth, is occurring.

Example problems

Problem 1
State the domain and range of the function y = x² + 5.

> The domain of the function is the set of all permissible x-values—in other words, all x-values that will yield a real y-value when plugged into the function. Any real number will yield a real number when squared, so the set of permissible values for x is the set of all real numbers.
>
> The range of the function is the set of all possible y-values the function can attain. There is a limit to the range of this function: if x is a real number, the value of x^2 can never be less than zero. Therefore, the value of $x^2 + 5$ can never be less than 5, so the range of the function is the set of all real numbers greater than or equal to 5.

Problem 2

Mariel has ten coins in her pocket. All of them are quarters and dimes, and their total value is $1.60. How many of each type of coin does she have?

To solve this problem, we can set up a system of two linear equations. If Q is the number of quarters and D is the number of dimes, we have:
$$D + Q = 10$$
$$10D + 25Q = 160$$
This system is solved most easily by substitution. The first equation can be rewritten as D = 10 – Q, and then the expression 10 – Q can be substituted for D in the second equation, giving us 10(10 – Q) + 25Q = 160. Solving:
$$10(10 - Q) + 25Q = 160$$
$$100 - 10Q + 25Q = 160$$
$$100 + 15Q = 160$$
$$15Q = 60$$
$$Q = 4$$
Mariel has 4 quarters.
Substituting 4 for Q in the first equation, we get D + 4 = 10, so D = 6. Mariel has 6 dimes.

Problem 3

State the domain and range of the function y = 2ln(x + 5).

The domain of the function y = ln x is the set of all positive real numbers, with a vertical exponent at x = 0. The range is the set of all real numbers.

Multiplying the natural log function by a constant does not affect the domain and range. However, adding a constant to the argument of the function does. The natural log function can only operate on positive numbers, but it operates on all positive numbers; therefore, the function y = 2ln(x + 5) exists for all values of x that make the quantity $(x + 5)$ greater than zero. That means that the domain of the function is the set of all real numbers greater than -5.

Problem 4

Solve the equation $2 \cdot (4)^x = (4)^{2x-2}$ for x. Does solving it become easier if we replace 4 with 2^2?

To solve the equation in its original form, first we take the $\log_4$ of both sides: $\log_4 (2 \cdot (4)^x) = \log_4 (4)^{2x-2}$. The left-hand side becomes $\log_4 (2) + \log_4 (4)^x$, or 0.5 + x; the right-hand side becomes simply 2x – 2. So we have x + 0.5 = 2x – 2; subtracting x from both sides and adding 2 to both sides, we get x = 2.5.

Replacing 4 with 2^2 requires us to multiply exponents; we end up with $2 \cdot (2)^{2x} = (2)^{4x-4}$. However, now we can simplify the left-hand side to $(2)^{2x+1}$; then we can take the $\log_2$ of both sides without having to deal with square roots or fractional logarithms. We end up with 2x + 1 = 4x – 4, or 2x = 5, which once again gives us x = 2.5.

Problem 5
Solve the inequality $3(\ln x) + 4 < 10$ for x.

The first step is to get the logarithm isolated on one side of the inequality. Subtracting 4 from both sides and dividing by 3 gives us $\ln x < 2$. Then, raising e to the power of both sides yields $x < e^2$. This value can be approximated as 7.389, or left as it is.

However, we also must consider the limited domain of the natural log function: it is only defined for positive values of x. This means that the solution to our inequality is not simply the set of real numbers less than e^2; instead it is the set of real numbers greater than 0 and less than e^2.

Problem 6
Marshall puts $1000 in a savings account that earns 4% interest compounded annually. How many years will it take for him to have at least $1200 in the account?

The formula that determines how much money will be in the account after y years is $m = 1000 \cdot 1.04^y$. We want to find the value of y for which m will be at least 1200, so we set up the inequality $1200 \leq 1000 \cdot 1.04^y$ and solve it for y.

Dividing both sides by 1000 gives us $1.2 \leq 1.04^y$; we then take the $\log_{1.04}$ of both sides to get $\log_{1.04}(1.2) \leq y$. To find this logarithm, we can use the change of base property: $\log_{1.04}(1.2) = \frac{\ln 1.2}{\ln 1.04}$. Plugging this into a calculator, we get approximately 4.6.

Since interest is compounded once a year, we round up: it will take at least 5 years for Marshall to have $1200.

Probability

Defining a random variable

In order to graph a random variable and analyze its distribution, it's helpful to quantify it, to assign a numerical value to each possible event. This is more useful when there is some number that naturally corresponds to the event, rather than just arbitrary assignments. If the random variable represents the colors of the cars passing by, there's little gained by defining 1 to correspond to blue, 2 to red, and so on. However, if you want to quantify a student's attendance in a class, for example, one can derive a suitable number by, perhaps, adding together the number of days the student has been absent plus one fourth the number of days he has been tardy. This then gives a numerical value that can be graphed and otherwise analyzed.

Probability distribution of a random variable

A probability distribution is a set of values of a random variable, with a probability assigned to each one. All possible values of the random variable should be represented in the distribution, and the sum of all their probabilities must equal 1, or 100%. For instance, suppose our random variable represents the number of tails that come up if we flip a coin five times. The probability that no tails will come up is $\frac{1}{2^5} = \frac{1}{32}$, the probability of one tails is $\frac{5}{32}$, the probability of two or three tails is each $\frac{5}{16}$, the probability of four tails is $\frac{5}{32}$, and the probability that the coin will come up heads all five times is $\frac{1}{32}$. Note that as required, the sum of all these probabilities is equal to 1: $\frac{1}{32} + \frac{5}{32} + \frac{5}{16} + \frac{5}{16} + \frac{5}{32} + \frac{1}{32} = \frac{1+5+10+10+5+1}{32} = \frac{32}{32} = 1$.

<u>Graphing</u>
A probability distribution of a random variable may be graphed similarly to a data set. You can plot the value of the variable on the x axis and the probability corresponding to that outcome on the y axis. Since the probabilities add to 1, the individual probabilities are likely to be small, and the axis should be scaled accordingly. For example, consider the random variable corresponding to the sum of the numbers on three fair dice. The probability that this sum will be 3 is $\frac{1}{216} \approx 0.0046$. The probability that the dice will sum to 4 is $\frac{3}{216} \approx 0.014$, and so on; the largest probabilities arise in the center, where we reach a probability of $\frac{27}{216} = 0.125$ that the sum of the dice will be 10, and the same probability for 11. If we plot the probabilities of each possible outcome on a graph, we get the following:

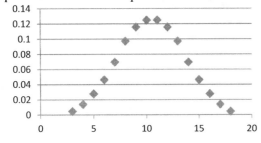

Sample space in which theoretical probabilities can be calculated

For a random variable in a sample space in which theoretical probabilities can be calculated, developing a probability distribution is just a matter of calculating the theoretical probabilities for each value of the variable, and then assigning each one to the appropriate variable.

For example, suppose there is a multiple choice test with five questions, each with four choices. The probability of a student guessing all five questions correctly is $\left(\frac{1}{4}\right)^5 \approx 0.00098$. The probability of his guessing four questions correctly is $\left(\frac{1}{4}\right)^4 \left(\frac{3}{4}\right) {}_5C_4 \approx 0.01465$. The chances of his guessing three questions correctly is $\left(\frac{1}{4}\right)^3 \left(\frac{3}{4}\right)^2 {}_5C_3 \approx 0.08789$, of guessing two questions correctly $\left(\frac{1}{4}\right)^2 \left(\frac{3}{4}\right)^3 {}_5C_2 \approx 0.26367$, of guessing one question $\left(\frac{1}{4}\right) \left(\frac{3}{4}\right)^4 {}_5C_1 \approx 0.39551$, and of his guessing all the questions incorrectly $\left(\frac{3}{4}\right)^5 \approx 0.23731$. If we define our random variable to be the number of questions that a student guesses correctly, then matching these probabilities to the corresponding values of the random variable gives us an appropriate probability distribution.

Sample space in which probabilities are assigned empirically

In developing a probability distribution for a sample space in which probabilities are assigned empirically, most of the work is done for you. You just have to define your random variable, and then assign to each value of the random variable the appropriate probability. For example, suppose that you find data on pet ownership in a particular neighborhood claiming that 22% of the neighborhood's households own no pets, 30% own one pet, 19% own two, 13% own three pets, 9% own four pets, 4% own five pets, 3% own six pets, and 1% own seven pets. A natural choice for a random variable is the number of pets owned by a particular household in the neighborhood. The corresponding probabilities are therefore just the quoted percentages, since these are equal to the probabilities that a randomly chosen household in the neighborhood will have that number of pets.

Expected value of a random variable

Probabilities of various outcomes are given

The expected value of a random variable is the sum of the possible values of the variable weighted by the probability of that value occurring. Mathematically, it can be expressed as $E(X) = \sum_{i=1}^{N} x_i P(x_i)$.

For instance, suppose you have a weighted die that has a probability $\frac{1}{3}$ of coming up 6, a probability $\frac{1}{6}$ of coming up 5, and a probability $\frac{1}{8}$ of coming up 1, 2, 3, or 4. The expected value of the die's result is therefore $6\left(\frac{1}{3}\right) + 5\left(\frac{1}{6}\right) + 4\left(\frac{1}{8}\right) + 3\left(\frac{1}{8}\right) + 2\left(\frac{1}{8}\right) + 1\left(\frac{1}{8}\right) = 2 + \frac{5}{6} + \frac{1}{2} + \frac{3}{8} + \frac{1}{4} + \frac{1}{8} = \frac{48+20+12+9+6+3}{24} = \frac{98}{24} = \frac{49}{12} \approx 4.08$.

Note that, as seen in this example, the expected value is not necessarily a value that you would actually expect to see; the weighted die will never show 4.08. Rather, it plays a role similar to the mean of a data set, providing a measure of central tendency of the variable's distribution.

Sample space in which theoretical probabilities can be calculated

The first step in finding the expected value of a random variable is to calculate the probabilities for each value. After that, we can find the expected value by summing all the possible values of the random variable, weighted by the respective probabilities, $E(X) = \sum_{i=1}^{N} x_i P(x_i)$.

For example, suppose there is a multiple choice test with five questions, each with four choices. We can set our random variable to be the number of questions a student guesses correctly. Without going into details of the calculations, the probability of a student guessing all five questions correctly is about 0.00098. The probability of his guessing four questions correctly is about 0.01465, three 0.08789, two 0.26367, one 0.39551, none 0.23731. The expected value for our random variable is therefore $E(X) = 5(0.00098) + 4(0.01465) + 3(0.08789) + 2(0.26367) + 1(0.39551) + 0(0.23731) = 1.25$—on average, we would expect a student to guess about one and one quarter questions correctly.

Sample space in which probabilities are assigned empirically

The first step is to define an appropriate probability distribution, which is just a matter of matching up the probabilities to the corresponding values of the variable. After that, you can find the expected value by just summing the possible values, weighted by their probabilities: $E(X) = \sum_{i=1}^{N} x_i P(x_i)$. For example, suppose that you find data on pet ownership in a particular neighborhood claiming that 22% of the neighborhood's households own no pets, 30% own one pet, 19% own two, 13% own three pets, 9% own four pets, 4% own five pets, 3% own six pets, and 1% own seven pets. The expected value for the number of pets in a household in the neighborhood is then (0)(0.22)+(1)(0.30)+(2)(0.19)+(3)(0.13)+(4)(0.09)+(5)(0.04)+(6)(0.03)+(7)(0.01)=1.88. The mean number of pets owned by a household in the neighborhood is 1.88; in 100 randomly selected households, you would expect to find a total of (100)(1.88) = 188 pets.

Mean of a probability distribution

The mean of a probability distribution is synonymous with the expected value of a random variable. It can be calculated by summing all possible values of the variable weighted by their respective probabilities, $E(X) = \sum_{i=1}^{N} x_i P(x_i)$. For a uniform distribution, with all probabilities the same, $P(x_i) = \frac{1}{N}$ for all I, and this reduces to $(X) = \frac{1}{N} \sum_{i=1}^{N} x_i$, the more familiar formula for the mean of a data set. The more general formula for the mean of a probability distribution, however, holds for arbitrary distributions that may not be uniform. The mean serves a similar role to the mean of a data set; it provides a measure of central tendency, and a rough idea of what a typical data point looks like. However, it also suffers from some of the same limitations as the mean of a data set, and does not by itself provide a complete picture of the distribution.

Expected payoff for a game of chance

The expected payoff for a game of chance is simply the expected value for a participant's winnings. This can be calculated the same way the expected value is calculated of any probability distribution: by summing all the possible values for the winnings together, weighted by their probability. For example, suppose a participant in a particular lottery has a one in ten million chance of winning a million dollars—and otherwise wins nothing. Then the expected payoff is equal to $\left(\frac{1}{10,000,000}\right)(\$1,000,000) + \left(\frac{9,999,999}{10,000,000}\right)(\$0) = \$0.10$.

For a more complicated example, suppose a particular game of chance has a 1 in 10 chance of paying off \$3, a 1 in 20 chance of paying \$5, and a 1 in 100 chance of paying \$20. Then the expected payoff is $\left(\frac{1}{10}\right)(\$3) + \left(\frac{1}{20}\right)(\$5) + \left(\frac{1}{100}\right)(\$20) = \$0.75$. (We omit this time writing down the term corresponding to a payoff of \$0, since the probability of this term doesn't affect the result anyway.)

Determining amount charged for a ticket in a game of chance

In order to make a profit on a sweepstake, raffle, lottery, or other game of chance, it's necessary for the charge for participation to be more than the expected payoff—otherwise, you're likely to pay out as much or more to winners than you bring in. Of course, the more the charge for tickets, the higher the profits, but setting the cost too high is likely to discourage people from entering.

For example, suppose that a particular raffle gives out one prize worth \$5000, five prizes worth \$1000, and twenty prizes worth \$100. If the organizers of the raffle expect to sell five thousand raffle tickets, then the expected payoff is equal to $\left(\frac{1}{5000}\right)(\$5000) + \left(\frac{5}{5000}\right)(\$1000) + \left(\frac{20}{5000}\right)(\$100) = \$2.40$. In order to make a profit, then, the organizers of the raffle have to charge more than \$2.40 for raffle tickets.

High chance of low payoff vs. low chance of high payoff

It is not always the case that a high chance of a low payoff is better than a low chance of a high payoff, or vice versa. To use probabilistic techniques to choose between a high chance of a low payoff and a low chance of a high payoff, it's necessary to compare the expected payoffs from each option. For instance, suppose you have a choice between a 10% chance of getting \$100, or a 1% chance of getting \$2,000. The expected payoff from the first option is $(0.1)(\$100) + (0.9)(\$0) = \$10$, while the expected payoff from the second option is $(0.01)(\$2000) + (0.99)(\$0) = \$20$. In this case, the higher-risk option is the better choice. On the other hand, if you have to choose between a 25% chance of getting \$100 or a 1% chance of getting \$2000, then the expected payoff from the first option is $(0.25)(\$100) + (0.75)(\$0) = \$25$, and the expected payoff from the second option is $(0.01)(\$2000) + (0.99)(\$0) = \$20$. In this case, the better choice is the lower-risk option.

Using probabilities to decide between insurance policies

To use probabilities to choose between insurance policies, you can calculate the expected net cost of each policy, depending on the estimated probability that the policy will be needed. Suppose you have a choice between two car insurance policies: one costs \$50 a month and pays \$1,000 in the case of a severe accident, while the other costs \$100 a month but pays \$4,000. If you estimate your chances in a given month of getting in a severe accident as 1 in 100, then the expected payoff for the first policy is $\left(\frac{1}{100}\right)(\$1000) = \$10$, minus the \$50 a month for a total monthly net cost of \$40. Similar calculations show that the second policy has an expected net monthly cost of \$60. The first policy, then, would be the better choice. However, if your chances of getting in an accident in a given month are 1 in 50, then the monthly cost of the first policy becomes \$30, and of the second \$20. Now the second policy is the better choice.

Using probabilities to decide between a number of options

A random decision may be considered "fair" if all outcomes are equally likely. To make a fair decision, therefore, it is necessary to choose a procedure that will make all outcomes equally likely. Analyzing a model using the laws of probability can help determine whether or not that model really gives rise to equally probable outcomes. For example, suppose it is necessary to randomly choose one of eleven people to receive some prize. One way that may come to mind is to roll two dice and sum the results. This yields a number between 2 and 12—eleven possible outcomes. However, these outcomes are *not* equally likely. The probability of rolling a 2 is only $\frac{1}{36}$, for example, but the probability of rolling a 7 is $\frac{1}{6}$—six times as likely! A procedure better suited to a fair decision would be drawing lots. For instance, eleven identical slips of paper could be labeled with the name of one of the possible outcomes, and one of the slips randomly drawn.

True random number generator

A true random number generator should produce all possible outcomes with equal probability. Therefore, one can test the random number generator by performing a large number of trials and examining the distribution of the results. If indeed all possible results do seem to appear with equal frequency, then the random number generator may be truly random. If some results appear with significantly greater frequency than others, then the random generator is faulty.

Technically, just the fact that the possible outcomes are equally likely does not necessarily make the random number generator random, however. Technically, for instance, it's possible for a random generator to produce all possible outcomes in a fixed order, cycling through them all before returning to the beginning of the sequence. Such a number generator would produce all outcomes with equal probability, but would not be random. Such cases may be more difficult to test for, but extreme examples like this one can often be easily spotted.

Using probability

Medical testing
Medical testing can be conducted by controlled experimental trials. Patients can be separated into several groups, some of which receive varying amounts of the medication or other treatment that is being tested, while the others receive a placebo (a substance with no effect so that the patients themselves do not know which are receiving the real treatment). Variables related to the effect of the treatment can then be observed and compared between the groups. Based on what we know about probability, there are some considerations that must be taken into account when conducting such a test. For one, the patients must be chosen and the groups assigned randomly, to avoid bias. If the groups are not initially similar to each other, then the difference in the results will not be meaningful. Also, before coming to conclusions based on the result, it is important to make sure that the differences between the groups are really significant, and that we do not assume that correlation proves causation.

Product market research

Market research is the practice of finding out what the public thinks about certain current or proposed products and services. This is usually done by means of a sample survey: it's impractical to survey every individual potential customer, so researchers choose a representative sample of possible customers and survey them as to their opinions on the product or service in question.

Based on what we know about probability, there are some considerations that must be taken into account when conducting such research. For one, the survey participants must be chosen randomly, to avoid bias. If the survey participants are all from a similar subset of the population, they may not be a representative sample of the whole population of potential customers, and the results from the survey may not extend to the population as a whole. Also, before coming to conclusions based on the result, it is important to make sure that the differences between the responses to different products are really significant.

When to change the goalie during a losing hockey game

If there seem to be a lot of goals scored on the goalie on a hockey team, it may be tempting to replace to goalie to improve the circumstance. However, this may not always be the best choice, and probability considerations may allow for more consideration of the matter. One thing to consider is that correlation does not prove causation: the fact that there are more goals being scored against this goalie doesn't mean it's the goalie's fault. Perhaps there's a third variable in action; could the other defensive players have been put in the same time as the goalie, and are they allowing more goals to reach him? It's also important to consider whether the apparent increase in the number of goals being scored is really significant, or whether it might just be the result of random fluctuation. Of course, similar principles apply not only to the case of switching out goalies in hockey games; these same considerations apply to a wide variety of real-life situations.

Statistical experiment

Sample space

The sample space of a statistical experiment is the set of all possible distinct outcomes of the experiment. If the experiment comprises the flip of a coin, for example, there are only two elements in the sample space: either the coin will come up heads, or the coin will come up tails. For the roll of a standard die, there are six possible outcomes in the sample space, one for each number that could come up on the die. When drawing a card from a full deck (without jokers), there are 52 possible outcomes. The elements of the sample space need not all have the same probability. If you roll a weighted die that comes up 1 50% of the time, the sample space is the same as for the roll of an ordinary, unweighted die; only the probabilities of the elements in the sample space differ.

Event

In a statistical experiment, an *event* can be defined as a subset of the sample space—that is, an event is a particular collection of possible outcomes. The event may have only one element, or it may have many different elements. For instance, suppose the statistical experiment in question is the draw of a card from a deck. One event is the draw of the ace of spades—this is one possible outcome from the draw. Another could be the draw of a jack—this event comprises four possible outcomes, since there are four jacks in the deck.

Still another could be the draw of a black card—twenty-six of the cards in the deck are black, so this event comprises twenty-six different outcomes.

Union and intersection of two sets of outcomes

Let A and B each be a set of elements or outcomes. Since the application is probability theory, we will use the term "outcomes". The union (symbol $\cup$) of two sets is the set of elements found in Set A or Set B. For example, if A={2,3,4} and B={3,4,5}, $A \cup B = \{2, 3, 4, 5\}$. Note that the outcomes 3 and 4 appear only once in the union. For statistical events, the union is equivalent to "or"; P(A $\cup$ B) is the same thing as P(A or B). The intersection (symbol $\cap$) of two sets is the set of outcomes common to both sets. For the above sets A and B, $A \cap B = \{3, 4\}$. For statistical events, the intersection is equivalent to "and"; P(A $\cap$ B) is the same thing as P(A and B). The union and intersection commute: $A \cup B = B \cup A$ and $A \cap B = B \cap A$. The union of sets is left and right distributive over intersection, $A \cup (B \cap C) = (A \cup B) \cap (A \cup C)$ and $(B \cap C) \cup A = (B \cup A) \cap (C \cup A)$. Likewise, the intersection of sets is left and right distributive over union: $A \cap (B \cup C) = (A \cap B) \cup (A \cap C)$ and $(B \cup C) \cap A = (B \cap A) \cup (C \cap A)$.

Complement of a set of outcomes

In general, the complement of a set is the set of all possible elements *not* in the set. This requires first defining the set of all possible elements under consideration, known as the *universe*. In probability theory, however, this is already defined; the universe under consideration is the sample space. The complement of a set of outcomes is therefore the set of all outcomes in the sample space that are *not* in the original set. For example, suppose that an integer is randomly chosen between 1 and 7. The sample space is then {1, 2, 3, 4, 5, 6, 7}. Consider the set of outcomes A = {1, 3, 4}. Then its complement A^C = {2, 5, 6, 7}—all the possible outcomes in the sample set that do not appear in A.

The complement of a union of two sets is the intersection of their complements, and vice versa: $(A \cup B)^C = A^C \cap B^C$, and $(A \cap B)^C = A^C \cup B^C$.

Events defined in terms of other events

Consider the draw of a card from a deck. Drawing the ace of spades is one possible event; drawing a red card is another; drawing a face card is still another. Still another event is the drawing of either the ace of spades *or* a red card—since both the outcomes of the two events "ace of spades" and "red card" are included, this event is the union of those two events. We can also consider drawing a red face card, i.e. a card that is both a red card *and* a face card. The set of outcomes in this event is the intersection of those in the two events "red card" and "face card". The drawing of a card that is *not* a face card is also an event, the complement of the face card event. In general, "or" indicates a union, "and" an intersection, and "not" a complement of events.

Two independent events

Two events are independent if the occurrence of one event has no effect on the probability of the other event occurring. For example, for two successive coin flips, the coin comes up heads on the first flip and the coin coming up heads on the second flip are independent events: whether the coin comes up heads or tails on the first flip has no effect on whether it comes up heads or tails on the second. However, if you draw two cards from a deck, while not replacing the first card, the probability of the first and second cards being red represents dependent events. In this case, the number of possible outcomes and the sample space, in the second event, are each decreased by 1.

Product of the probabilities to prove independence

For two independent events, and *only* for independent events, the product of the probabilities of each event is equal to the probability that both events will occur: $P(A)P(B) = P(A \cap B)$. If we know these probabilities, then, we can use this equation to check whether the events are independent. Conversely, if we know the probabilities of two events that we know are independent, we can use this equation to find the probability that both will occur. For example, suppose you're programming a computer game in which there's a random chance of finding a certain item at the end of each level. You want the chances at each level to be independent. Suppose you find after running some trials that the chances of finding the item at the end of the first level are $\frac{1}{3}$, at the end of the second level are $\frac{1}{4}$, and at the end of both the first *and* the second level are $\frac{1}{12}$. Since $\left(\frac{1}{3}\right)\left(\frac{1}{4}\right) = \left(\frac{1}{12}\right)$, this proves that the events are indeed independent.

Conditional probability

Given two events A and B, the conditional probability P(A|B) is the probability that event B will occur, given that event A has occurred. For instance, suppose you have a jar containing two red marbles and two blue marbles, and you draw two marbles at random. Note. The first drawn marble is not replaced. Consider event A being the event that the first marble drawn is red, and event B being the event that the second marble drawn is blue. With no conditions set, both P(A) and P(B) are equal to $\frac{1}{2}$. However, if we know that the first marble drawn was red—that is, that event A occurred—then that leaves one red marble and two blue marbles in the jar. In that case, the probability that the second marble is blue given that the first marble was red—that is, P(A|B)—is equal to $\frac{2}{3}$.

Calculation of the conditional probability $P(A|B)$ in terms of the probabilities of events A and B and their union and/or intersection

The conditional probability $P(A|B)$ is the probability that event B will occur given that event A occurs. This cannot be calculated simply from $P(A)$ and $P(B)$; these probabilities alone do not give sufficient information to determine the conditional probability. It can, however, be determined given also $P(A \cap B)$, the probability that events A and B both occur. Specifically, $P(A|B) = \frac{P(A \cap B)}{P(B)}$.

For instance, suppose you have a jar containing two red marbles and two blue marbles, and you draw two marbles at random. Consider event A being the event that the first marble drawn is red, and event B being the event that the *second* marble drawn is blue. *P(A)* is $\frac{1}{2}$, and $P(A \cap B)$ is $\frac{1}{3}$. (The latter may not be obvious, but may be determined by finding the product of $\frac{1}{2}$ and $\frac{2}{3}$.) Therefore $P(A|B) = \frac{1/3}{1/2} = \frac{2}{3}$.

<u>What the fact that two events A and B are independent implies about the conditional probability P(A|B)</u>

The conditional probability $P(A|B)$ is the probability that event B will occur given that event A occurs. If the two events are independent, we do not expect that whether or not event A occurs should have any effect on whether or not event B occurs. In other words, we expect $P(A|B)=P(A)$.

This can be proven using the usual equations for conditional probability and the joint probability of independent events. The conditional probability $P(A|B) = \frac{P(A \cap B)}{P(B)}$. But if A and B are independent, then $P(A \cap B) = P(A)P(B)$. So $P(A|B) = \frac{P(A)P(B)}{P(B)} = P(A)$. By similar reasoning, if A and B are independent then $P(B|A)=P(B)$.

Determining independence from a two-way frequency table

If we have a two-way frequency table, it is generally a straightforward matter to read off the probabilities of any two events A and B, as well as the joint probability of both events occurring, $P(A \cap B)$. We can then check whether or not the events are independent by verifying whether $P(A)P(B) = P(A \cap B)$.

For example, consider the following table, showing a certain store's recent T-shirt sales, categorized by size and color:

		Size			
		Small	Medium	Large	Total
	Blue	25	40	35	100
Color	White	27	25	22	74
	Black	8	23	15	26
	Total	60	88	72	220

Suppose we want to check whether the event A that a customer buys a blue shirt is independent of the event B that a customer buys a medium shirt. From the table, $P(A) = \frac{100}{220} = \frac{5}{11}$ and $P(B) = \frac{88}{220} = \frac{4}{10}$. Also, $P(A \cap B) = \frac{40}{220} = \frac{2}{11}$. Since $\left(\frac{5}{11}\right)\left(\frac{4}{10}\right) = \frac{20}{220} = \frac{2}{11}$, $P(A)P(B) = P(A \cap B)$ and these two events are indeed independent.

Estimation of conditional probability from a two-way frequency table

If we have a two-way frequency table, it is generally a straightforward matter to read off the probabilities of any two events A and B, as well as the joint probability of both events occurring, $P(A \cap B)$. We can then find the conditional probability $P(A|B)$ by calculating $P(A|B) = \frac{P(A \cap B)}{P(B)}$.

For example, a certain store's recent T-shirt sales:

		Size			
		Small	Medium	Large	Total
Color	Blue	25	40	35	100
	White	27	25	22	74
	Black	8	23	15	26
	Total	60	88	72	220

Suppose we want to find the conditional probability that a customer buys a black shirt (event A), given that the shirt he buys is size small (event B). From the table, the probability $P(A)$ that a customer buys a small shirt is $\frac{60}{220} = \frac{3}{11}$. The probability $P(A \cap B)$ that he buys a small, *black* shirt is $\frac{8}{220} = \frac{2}{55}$. The conditional probability $P(A|B)$ that he buys a black shirt, given that he buys a small shirt, is therefore $P(A|B) = \frac{2/55}{3/11} = \frac{2}{15}$.

Applications of conditional probability in everyday situations

Conditional probability often arises in everyday situations in, for example, estimating the risk or benefit of certain activities. The conditional probability of having a heart attack given that you exercise daily may be smaller than the overall probability of having a heart attack. The conditional probability of having lung cancer given that you are a smoker is larger than the overall probability of having lung cancer. Note that changing the order of the conditional probability changes the meaning: the conditional probability of having lung cancer given that you are a smoker is a very different thing from the probability of being a smoker given that you have lung cancer. In an extreme case, suppose that a certain rare disease is caused only by eating a certain food, but even then is unlikely. Then the conditional probability of having that disease given that you eat the dangerous food is nonzero but low, but the conditional probability of having eaten that food given that you have the disease is 100%!

Applications of independence of events in everyday situations

Even if we don't necessarily think of it in those terms, we often use independence of events in everyday situations. We know when playing a board game, for instance, that each roll of the die is independent, and is unaffected by previous rolls. Sometimes, however, our intuition fails us and we tend to think of independent events as influencing each other; if we flip a coin and it comes up heads three times in a row, we may erroneously believe on some level that the next flip is more likely to come up tails because a tails is "overdue". Many gamblers make this mistake, seeing meaningful streaks in random results, and expecting certain results on the basis of previous events. Remembering what it means for events to be random helps avoid this error.

Uniform probability model

A uniform probability model is a model in which the probabilities of all outcomes are equally likely. For example, the roll of a fair die can be simulated by such a model; it's equally likely that any face of the die come up on top. Likewise, the draw of a card from a well-shuffled deck can be represented by a uniform probability model; it's equally likely for any card to be drawn.

One useful feature of a uniform probability model is that probabilities can be determined by simply counting outcomes. The probability of an event A occurring is equal to the total number of outcomes in event A divided by the total number of outcomes in the sample set. For example, suppose we want to know the probability of drawing a face card from a well-shuffled deck of cards (without jokers). There are fifty-two cards in the deck, twelve of which are face cards. The probability of drawing a face card from the deck is therefore $\frac{12}{52} = \frac{3}{13}$. When plotted, a uniform distribution is rather flat, in appearance. A uniform distribution results, when plotting the sampling distribution of a large number of samples, thus illustrating the Central Limit Theorem.

<u>Find the conditional probability $P(A|B)$ given all possible outcomes included in event B, without necessarily having to take into account the entire sample space</u>

Although one way of finding the conditional probability is to calculate $P(A|B) = \frac{P(A \cap B)}{P(B)}$, this is not the only way. For a uniform probability model, it's possible to find the conditional probability even without knowing the overall probability of any event, just knowing all the outcomes included in event B. To see this, consider that the probability of event B occurring is equal to the number of outcomes in event B, which we can call X_B, divided by the total number of outcomes in the sample space, X_{TOTAL}. Similarly, the probability of events A and B both occurring is equal to the number of outcomes in the intersection of A and B, $X_{A \cap B}$, divided by the total number of outcomes in the sample space, X_{TOTAL}. So the conditional probability $P(A|B) = \frac{P(A \cap B)}{P(B)} = \frac{X_{A \cap B}/X_{TOTAL}}{X_B/X_{TOTAL}} = \frac{X_{A \cap B}}{X_B}$. In other words, we can find the conditional probability $P(A|B)$ by simply dividing the number of outcomes that belong to both A and B by the number of outcomes that belong to B: $P(A|B)$ is the fraction of B's outcomes that also belong to A.

<u>Interpreting a conditional probability</u>
A conditional probability $P(A|B)$ is the probability that event A will occur given that event B occurs. For a uniform probability model, this is equal to the fraction of B's outcomes that also belong to A. For instance, suppose we are interested in knowing the number of students of each grade at a certain school who buy their lunch at the school and who take their lunch from home. We will call the event that a randomly chosen student is in the ninth grade event A, and the event that he buys his lunch at school event B. Since the students are randomly chosen with equal probability, this is a uniform probability model. The probability that a student buys his lunch at school, given that he is in the ninth grade, is $P(A|B)$, and is simply equal to the fraction of ninth-grade students who buy their lunches at the school.

<u>Interpreting the result of the addition rule</u>
The addition rule states that $P(A \cup B) = P(A) + P(B) - P(A \cap B)$. The result of the equation gives the probability that either event A or B will occur, which for a uniform probability distribution is equal to the fraction of outcomes in either A or B.

Suppose, for example, we are told that of the books on a certain shelf, $\frac{1}{3}$ are paperbacks, $\frac{1}{2}$ are fiction, and $\frac{1}{4}$ are paperback fiction books. We can call event A the event that a randomly chosen book is a paperback and event B the event that a randomly chosen book is fiction.

Since we are randomly choosing the books, this is a uniform probability model. From the given information, $P(A) = \frac{1}{3}$, $P(B) = \frac{1}{2}$, and $P(A \cap B)$—the probability that a randomly chosen book is both paperback *and* fiction—is equal to $\frac{1}{4}$. So $P(A \cup B) = \frac{1}{3} + \frac{1}{2} - \frac{1}{4} = \frac{7}{12}$. This indicates in this case that $\frac{7}{12}$ of the books are either paperback or fiction.

<u>Interpreting the result of the general multiplication rule</u>
The general multiplication rule states that $P(A \cap B) = P(A)P(B|A) = P(B)P(A|B)$. The result of this rule is the probability that events A and B will both occur, which for a uniform probability model is equal to the fraction of outcomes that are in both events A and B. For example, suppose we are told that $\frac{1}{4}$ of the insects in a certain woman's insect collection are butterflies, and that $\frac{1}{5}$ of those butterflies are blue. We can call event A the event that a randomly chosen insect from the collection is a butterfly and event B the event that it is blue. So $P(A) = \frac{1}{4}$, and $P(B|A) = \frac{1}{5}$—the fraction of butterflies in the collection that are blue is equal to the probability that a randomly chosen insect in the collection is blue, given that it is a butterfly. Then by the multiplication rule, $P(A \cap B) = P(A)P(B|A) = \left(\frac{1}{4}\right)\left(\frac{1}{5}\right) = \frac{1}{20}$. So the probability that a randomly selected insect from the collection is both blue and a butterfly is $\frac{1}{20}$; $\frac{1}{20}$ of the insects are blue butterflies.

Addition rule for probabilities

The addition rule for probabilities is $P(A \cup B) = P(A) + P(B) - P(A \cap B)$. In other words, the probability that either event A or event B will occur is equal to the sum of the probabilities of each event, minus the probability that they will both occur.
For example, suppose you want to find the probability that, when you roll two dice, either their numbers will match (event A) or they will add to eight (event B). $P(A) = \frac{6}{36} = \frac{1}{6}$, since there are six possible combinations of matching dice ((1,1), (2,2), (3,3), (4,4), (5,5), or (6,6)), and thirty-six combinations total. $P(B) = \frac{5}{36}$; there are five combinations that add to 8 ((2,6), (3,5), (4,4), (5,3), or (6,2)). $P(A \cap B) = \frac{1}{36}$; there is only one combination of matching dice that add to 8 (that is, (4,4)). So $P(A \cup B) = \frac{1}{6} + \frac{5}{36} - \frac{1}{36} = \frac{5}{18}$.

General multiplication rule

The general multiplication rule for probabilities states that $P(A \cap B) = P(A)P(B|A) = P(B)P(A|B)$. In other words, the probability that events A and B will both occur is equal to the probability that event A will occur times the probability that event B will occur on the condition that A occurs; or, equivalently, it is equal to the to the probability that event B will occur times the probability that event A will occur on the condition that B occurs. For example, suppose we're told that a certain cat is in a certain yard half the time, and when it is in the yard there is a $\frac{1}{3}$ chance that a second cat will be with it. We will call the event of the first cat being in the yard A, and the event of the second cat being in the yard B. Then from the given information, $P(A) = \frac{1}{2}$ and $P(B|A) = \frac{1}{3}$. The probability that both cats are in the yard is then $P(A \cap B) = P(A)P(B|A) = \left(\frac{1}{2}\right)\left(\frac{1}{3}\right) = \frac{1}{6}$.

- 79 -

Permutation

A permutation is a way of selecting k elements out of a larger group of n elements, in which the order matters: $(1, 2, 3)$ is considered a different permutation from $(2, 3, 1)$. The number of permutations of k elements out of n can be written as $_nP_k$, and is equal to $\frac{n!}{(n-k)!}$. When k is small, this is more easily calculated as $(n)(n-1)\ldots(n-k+1)$. For instance, there are six possible ways to choose two (ordered) elements out of three: $(1, 2), (2, 1), (1, 3), (3, 1), (2, 3), (3, 2)$. And, accordingly, $_3P_2 = \frac{3!}{(3-2)!} = \frac{6}{1} = 6$. The number of ways to choose five (ordered) elements out of a hundred is much harder to enumerate, but not hard to calculate: $_{100}P_5 = \frac{100!}{(100-5)!} = (100)(99)(98)(97)(96) = 9{,}034{,}502{,}400$. The number of ways to choose 95 (ordered) elements out of 100 is much larger, equal to $_{100}P_{95} = \frac{100!}{(100-95)!} = \frac{100!}{5!}$, which turns out to be a number with more than 150 digits.

A permutation can be used to solve a problem that involves finding the probability of one or more particular ordered arrangements of elements occurring. The permutation can be used to find the total number of outcomes in the sample space, and then the probability is the number of outcomes in the event in question divided by that number. For example, suppose you had twelve tiles labeled with the numbers one through twelve, and you wanted to find the probability that, if you drew three tiles at random, they would be consecutive numbers in ascending order. There are ten arrangements that fit those criteria: $(1, 2, 3), (2, 3, 4), (3, 4, 5), (4, 5, 6), (5, 6, 7), (6, 7, 8), (7, 8, 9), (8, 9, 10), (9, 10, 11)$, and $(10, 11, 12)$. The total number of possible outcomes is $_{12}P_3 = \frac{12!}{(12-3)!} = 1320$. The probability that they will fulfill the criteria is then $\frac{10}{1320} = \frac{1}{132}$.

Combination

A combination is a way of selecting k elements out of a larger group of n elements, in which the order doesn't matter: $(1, 2, 3)$ and $(2, 3, 1)$ are considered the same combination. The number of permutations of k elements out of n can be written as $_nC_k$, and is equal to $\frac{n!}{k!(n-k)!}$. For instance, there are three possible ways to choose two (unordered) elements out of three: $(1, 2), (2, 3),$ or $(1, 3)$. And, accordingly, $_3C_2 = \frac{3!}{2!(3-2)!} = \frac{6}{2 \cdot 1} = 3$. The number of ways to choose five (unordered) elements out of a hundred is much harder to enumerate, but not hard to calculate: $_{100}C_5 = \frac{100!}{5!(100-5)!} = \frac{100!}{5! \cdot 95!} = 75{,}287{,}520$. Similarly, the number of ways to choose 95 (unordered) elements out of 100 is equal to $_{100}C_{95} = \frac{100!}{95!(100-95)!} = \frac{100!}{95! \cdot 5!} = 75{,}287{,}520$. This illustrates a general rule: $_nC_k = {_n}C_{n-k}$, for any positive integer values of n and k such that $k \leq n$.

A combination can be used to solve a problem that involves finding the probability of one or more particular unordered arrangements of elements occurring. The combination can be used to find the total number of outcomes in the sample space, and then the probability is the number of outcomes in the event in question divided by that number. For example, suppose you wanted to find the probability of drawing a royal flush (a ten, ace, jack, queen, and king all of the same suit) from a standard deck of 52 cards. There are four suits in a standard deck, thus four possible royal flushes. Since the order of the cards doesn't matter, the total number of possible outcomes—sets of five cards that can be drawn—is equal to $_{52}C_5 = \frac{52!}{5!(52-5)!} = 2{,}598{,}960$. The probability of drawing a royal flush is therefore $\frac{4}{2{,}598{,}960} = \frac{1}{649{,}740}$.

Permutations and combinations when computing the probability of a compound event

Both combinations and permutations are used when it is required to determine the number of ways that k elements can be chosen (without repetition) out of a larger set of n elements. In general, a permutation is used when the order of the elements matters, and a combination when it doesn't. For instance, if we wanted to calculate how many different five-letter sequences are possible (with no letters repeated), the order matters, so we would want the *permutation* of five elements out of the twenty-six-letter alphabet, $_{26}P_5$ (which is equal to $\frac{26!}{(26-5)!} = 7{,}893{,}600$). If we wanted to calculate how many different hands of four cards we could draw from a deck of 52 cards, the order doesn't matter, so we would want the *combination* of four elements out of the fifty-two, $_{52}C_4$ (which is equal to $\frac{52!}{4!(52-4)!} = 270{,}725$.

Formulas for permutations and combinations

The number of permutations of k elements out of n, $_nP_k$, is equal to the number of ways we can choose k elements, in order, from a larger set of n. The first element can be any of the n elements of the larger set. Once we've chosen it, however, there are only $n - 1$ elements left to choose for the second element, then $n - 2$ for the third, and so on down to $n - k + 1$ for the kth element. The total number of possibilities is then the product of all of these numbers, $n(n - 1)(n - 2) \ldots (n - k + 1)$, which is equal to $\frac{n(n-1)(n-2)\ldots(n-k+1)(n-k)(n-k-1)\ldots(2)(1)}{(n-k)(n-k-1)\ldots(2)(1)} = \frac{n!}{(n-k)!}$.

The number of combinations of k elements out of n, $_nC_k$, is equal to the number of ways we can choose k elements out of a larger set of n, disregarding the order. This is similar to $_nP_k$ except that the order doesn't matter. Essentially, then, we can get $_nP_k$ from $_nC_k$ by multiplying by the number of possible orders of the k elements, which is $_kP_k = k!$. So $_nP_k = {_nC_k} \cdot k!$; solving for $_nC_k$ we get $_nC_k = \frac{_nP_k}{k!} = \frac{n!}{k!(n-k)!}$.

Calculating the number of possible sequences of six letters, with no letters repeated

The total number of possible sequences of six letters, with no letters repeated, is equal to the number of permutations of 6 elements out of 26, or $_{26}P_6$. This can be calculated as $_{26}P_6 = \frac{26!}{(26-6)!} = \frac{26!}{20!} = 165{,}765{,}600$. There are almost 166 million possible sequences of six letters, with no letters repeated. If repetitions are allowed, then the permutation formula no longer applies. Rather, now each letter can be treated as an independent event, since choosing one letter has no bearing on the possible choices for the others. Since there are 26 possible choices for the first letter, 26 for the second, 26 for the third, and so on, the total number of combinations is $26 \cdot 26 \cdot 26 \cdot 26 \cdot 26 \cdot 26 = 26^6 = 308{,}915{,}776$.

Data Analysis

Statistics

Statistics may be descriptive or inferential, in nature. Descriptive statistics does not involve inferences and includes measures of center and spread, frequencies, and percentages. Inferential statistics involves the process of making inferences about large populations based on the characteristics of random samples from the population. This field of statistics is useful because, for large populations, it may be impractical or impossible to measure the characteristics of each element of the population and determine the distributions of various properties exactly. By applying statistical methods, it's possible to make reasonable inferences about the distributions of a variable, or variables, throughout large populations by only examining a relatively small part of it. Of course, it's important that this be a "representative sample", that is, one in which the distribution of the variables of interest is similar to its distribution in the entire population. For this reason, it's desirable to create random samples, rather than choosing a set of similar samples.

Determining consistency of a specified model

One way to determine whether a model is consistent with a given data-generating process is to repeatedly run the process, or a simulation of the process, and examine the distribution of the results, comparing them with the distribution of the model. If the distribution of the experimental or simulated results seem to have a similar shape, center, and spread to that predicted by the model, then the model is consistent with the process. If there is a significant discrepancy, then the model is not consistent with the results. For instance, suppose you want to test whether a die is fair. This implies a model in which each number is equally likely to come up on the die. You could test this by rolling the die repeatedly and checking that indeed the numbers do come up approximately the same number of times. The distribution of the results from this experiment, when plotted, should be approximately normal.

When testing the consistency of a model, it's important to use a large number of trials in order to minimize the results of small random fluctuations. For small numbers of data points, small errors or coincidental runs of data may throw off the results and lead to false conclusions. With large amounts of data, significant deviations from the expected results become increasingly unlikely, and a match or mismatch with a model becomes increasingly likely to be significant. For instance, suppose you want to test whether a die is fair. If you roll the die three times and it comes up 1 every time, this may seem to be inconsistent with the model, and may lead to the conclusion that the die is unfair. However, for such a small number of trials, it's not too unlikely that this anomalous result occurred by chance. If you roll the die a thousand times and it comes up 1 five hundred times, then you can be much more confident that the die is unfair.

Sample surveys, experiments, and observational studies

Sample survey
A sample survey consists of obtaining data from a subset of the population. The data are a measure of a variable. The entire population does not need to be included in the study, but

to obtain the most accurate measure of the mean requires sampling without bias, since bias will shift the estimated value of the mean. When the variable being measured has different centers and/or spreads for its subsets, a more accurate estimate of the mean and the variance of the population can be obtained by a method called stratification, wherein the population is divided into more homogeneous subsets and the sample selected contains the same proportion of each subset as contained in the population. The number of data points in the sample must only be large enough to obtain estimates of the parameters within pre-determined confidence intervals.

In a well-conducted sample survey, the mean of a given variable within the surveyed sample should be approximately equal to the mean of the population as a whole. The same is true of the proportion of the sample to have a given variable within a particular range: this should be approximately equal to the proportion of the population as a whole with the variable in this range.

For instance, suppose that in a sample survey of a thousand mature animals of a particular species, the sampled individuals have an average mass of 21 kilograms, and five percent of the animals in the sample have a mass of more than 30 kilograms. Assuming that this is a well-conducted survey with a suitably chosen random sample, we would then expect the mean mass of all mature animals of the species to be 21 kilograms, and five percent of all mature animals of the species to have a mass of more than 30 kilograms.

Experiment
An experiment is a procedure by which the experimenter controls one or more "controlled variables" and then records one or more "observations". In an experiment, a treatment or intervention, is given. The general purpose of an experiment is to determine the causal relationship, if any, between variables. The simplest form of an experiment involves data with two variables (X, Y), where X is the *controlled variable* and Y is the *observation*. Generally, a function is "fitted" to the data so that it predicts the value of Y when given the value of X. The function is of the form, $\hat{y}=f(x)$, where $\hat{y}$ is the predicted value of the observation, Y, for a given value x of the controlled variable, X. For example, suppose $\hat{y} = f(x) = 3 + 4x$. In one run of the experiment, $(x_2, y_2) = (2,10.5)$, so $\hat{y} = 3 + 4(2) = 11$ and the *residual* is "observed value" – "predicted value" $= 10.5 - 11.0 = -0.5$.

Observational study
An observational study is a procedure in which a researcher examines/observes an individual, or group, . A set of a priori questions may or may not be used in the study. With observational studies, the researcher(s) does not interfere with the research process, by way of given treatments. The goal is for the researcher to have little or no influence on the naturally occurring process.

Differences
Sample surveys, experiments, and observations are all ways of measuring variables within a population. A sample survey simply polls a sample of the population and asks a set of Likert-scale and/or open-ended questions.. An experiment often seeks to find a relationship between variables. In this type of study, treatment and control groups are employed Experiments are especially useful to test specific models, to see whether the experimental results match those predicted by the model. There may be circumstances, however, when it's not possible to directly control the variables of interest, either for practical or for moral reasons. In this case, an observational study may be conducted, in

which one observes an individual or group, within a population, without having any direct impact on the included variables.

Role of randomization

Randomization is important in sample surveys, experiments, and observational studies to avoid bias. In a sample survey, for instance, if the surveyor surveys only his acquaintances or some other handpicked group, he may exhibit an unconscious bias toward individuals with certain properties, distorting his results. A random selection from the population minimizes bias, though if the population comprises discrete subsets with different characteristics it may be best to randomly select individuals within each subset, the number from each subset proportional to the total size of the subset. Similarly, in experiments and observational studies, the experimental or observational subjects should be chosen randomly, subject to the parameters of the experiment.

Margin of error of a random sampling

The margin of error of a random sampling is the expected discrepancy between the mean and other characteristics of the variables in the random sampling, and those in the entire population. Generally, the larger the random sample relative to the entire population, the smaller the margin of error, to an extreme of a margin of error of zero when the sample comprises the entire population.

A margin of error can be estimated through a simulation, by setting up data set similar to the expected data in the population to be sampled, and then simulating choosing a sample of that data. By repeating this procedure, each time comparing the means of the variables as extrapolated from the sample to those of the entire simulated population, one can get a good idea of the margin of error to expect.

Using data from a randomized experiment to compare two treatments

A randomized experiment can be useful to compare two treatments to see which, if either, is more effective. If one group of patients is given one treatment and one given another, then variables related to whatever effect the treatment is supposed to produce can be measured and compared between the two groups—for instance, if the treatment is intended to cure a particular disease, then if each of two groups of inflicted patients are given one of the treatments, their rates of recovery can be measured and compared. To ensure that the treatments have any effect at all, the treated groups should also be compared against a group that is not given any treatment. In fact, to eliminate any psychosomatic effects from the patients knowing they are being treated, they should also be compared with a control group given a placebo with no actual medicinal effect.

Using simulations to validate experiment findings

The fact that the parameters of two groups in an experimental study are different does not necessarily mean that this difference is a product of the difference in the control variables. Some variation inevitably occurs, and it could be that the difference is simply the result of such statistical error. One way to test this is to use a two-sample z-test. Hypothesis testing will reveal a p-value that may be compared to an a priori level of significance. For a p-value less than the stated level of significance, the means of the two groups may be determined to be statistically different. (In this case, the null hypothesis of no difference, would be rejected.) Repeated studies, may be used to validate findings.

Using data to evaluate reports

Reports of results of trials and experiments generally include relationships and conclusions inferred from the experimental data. However, some reports may make faulty inferences and come to conclusions not justified by the data. To evaluate a report, it helps to check the data yourself and see if the conclusions stated are really warranted by the data. There are a number of questions to look out for. Did the writer of the report assume that correlation implied causation? Did he draw definitive conclusions from an apparent result that is too small to be significant? Did he randomly choose the samples for his experiment or survey, or did he select them in a way that might lead to possible bias? These are among the common mistakes to look out for, both in drawing conclusions from a study yourself and in evaluating a report written by someone else.

Dot plot, histogram, and box plot

Dot plots, histograms, and box plots are three different methods of representing data sets in graphical form. While they all have similar purposes, some are more suitable for some data sets than others. Dot plots represent each data point as a separate dot, and are most useful for relatively small data sets with a small number of possible values. When the data set contains more than a few dozen points, dot plots may become unwieldy. For larger data sets, where the data distribution is continuous rather than discrete, histograms may be more practical. Histograms are especially useful to estimate the *density* of the data, and to estimate probability density functions. Box plots may be used to summarize the shape of a larger number of univariate data values; they are most useful for comparing separate groups of data, such as the results of several different experiments, or the statistics of several discrete populations.

Dot plot
A dot plot is a representation of a data set in which each data point is represented by a dot or similar marking, with matching data points grouped in columns. For instance, the data set {2, 1, 3, 1, 1, 5, 4, 4, 3, 3, 3, 4, 1, 5} can be represented as a dot plot as follows:

For large data sets, it is possible for each dot in a dot plot to represent more than one data point. However, for such data sets other representations may be more suitable.

Histogram

A histogram is a representation of a data set in which the data are represented by bars corresponding to discrete intervals, with the height of each bar representative of the number of data points falling in the corresponding interval. For example, the data set {101, 141, 105, 159, 122, 107, 145, 153, 183, 172, 164, 162, 144, 132, 138, 116, 155, 147, 141, 129, 168, 145, 152} can be represented by a histogram as follows:

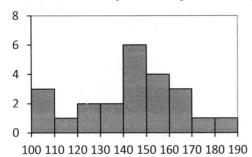

Histograms are useful for large data sets with values that may range continuously over intervals rather than being confined to discrete possibilities.

Box plot

A *box plot*, or box-and-whisker plot, is a representation of one or more data sets in which each data set is represented by a box with a bar in the middle and a "whisker" on each side. The bar represents the *median* of the data, and the edges of the box represent the first and third quartiles. The ends of the whiskers may represent the maximum and minimum data values, although often outliers are excluded and are represented instead as discrete points.

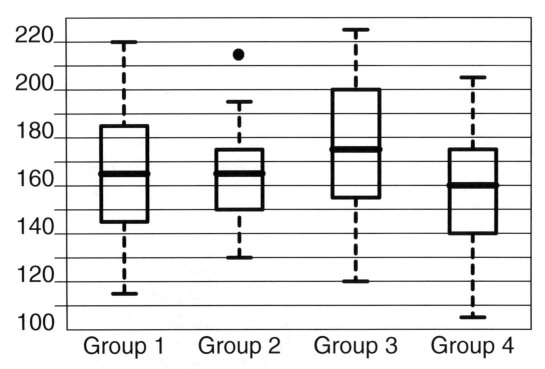

For example, given the data, 5, 5, 6, 9, 12, 14, 15, 17, 17, 21, 24, 26, 29, 31, 36, 38, 39, 46, 47, 49, the following summary statistics may be recorded: Median = 22.5, Q1 = 13, Q3 = 37, minimum = 5, and maximum = 49. Thus, a box plot of this data will show a box, with a middle bar at the value, 22.5, edges of the box at the values, 13 and 37, and whiskers at the values, 5 and 49. Box plots are useful when it is desired to compare the statistics of multiple related data sets, such as several different groups of experimental subjects.

Mean

The mean is the average of the data points; that is, it is the sum of the data points divided by the number of data points. Mathematically, the mean of a set of data points $\{x_1, x_2, x_3, \dots x_n\}$ can be written as $\bar{X} = \sum \frac{X}{N}$. For instance, for the data set $(1, 3, 6, 8, 100, 800)$, the mean is $\frac{1+3+6+8+100+800}{6} = 153$.

The mean is most useful, when data is approximately normal and does not include extreme outliers. In the above example, the data shows much variation. Thus, the mean is not the best measure of central tendency to use, when interpreting the data. With this data set, the median will give a more complete picture of the distribution.

Median

The median is the value in the middle of the data set, in the sense that 50% of the data points lie above the median and 50% of the data points lie below. The median can be determined by simply putting the data points in order, and selecting the data point in the middle. If there is an even number of data points, then the median is the average of the middle two data points. For instance, for the data set $\{1, 3, 6, 8, 100, 800\}$, the median is $\frac{6+8}{2} = 7$.

For distributions with widely varying data points, especially those with large outliers, the median is a more appropriate measure of central tendency, and thus gives a better idea of a "typical" data point. Notice in the data set above, the mean is 153, while the median is 7.

Mode

The mode is the value that appears most often in the data set. For instance, for the data set $\{2, 6, 4, 9, 4, 5, 7, 6, 4, 1, 5, 6, 7, 5, 6\}$, the mode is 6: the number 6 appears four times in the data set, while the next most frequent values, 4 and 5, appear only three times each. It is possible for a data set to have more than one mode: in the data set $\{11, 14, 17, 16, 11, 17, 12, 14, 17, 14, 13\}$, 14 and 17 are both modes, appearing three times each. In the extreme case of a uniform distribution—a distribution in which all values appear with equal probability—*all* values in the data set are modes.

The mode is useful to get a general sense of the shape of the distribution; it shows where the peaks of the distribution are. More information is necessary to get a more detailed description of the full shape.

First quartile

The first quartile of a data set is a value greater than or equal to one quarter of the data points (and less than the other three quarters). Various methods exist for defining the first quartile precisely; one of the simplest is to define the first quartile as the median of the first half of the ordered data (excluding the median if there are an odd number of data points). Applying this method, for example, to the data set $\{3, 1, 12, 7, 17, 4, 10, 8, 9, 20, 4\}$, we proceed as follows: Putting the data in order, we get $\{1, 3, 4, 4, 7, 8, 9, 10, 12, 17, 20\}$. The first half (excluding the median) is {1, 3, 4, 4, 7}, which has a median of 4. Therefore the first quartile of this data set is 4.

Third quartile

The third quartile of a data set is a value greater than or equal to three quarters of the data points (and less than the remaining quarter). Various methods exist for defining the third quartiles precisely; one of the simplest is to define the third quartile as the median of the second half of the ordered data (excluding the median if there are an odd number of data points).
Applying this method, for example, to the data set {3, 1, 12, 7, 17, 4, 10, 8, 9, 20, 4}, we proceed as follows: Putting the data in order, we get {1, 3, 4, 4, 7, 8, 9, 10, 12, 17, 20}. The second half (excluding the median) is {9, 10, 12, 17, 20}, which has a median of 12. Therefore the third quartile of this data set is 12.

Interquartile range

The interquartile range of a data set is the difference between the third and first quartiles. That is, one quarter of the data fall below the interquartile range and one quarter of the data above it. Exactly half of the data points fall within the interquartile range, half of those above the median and half below. (This is, of course, why the quartile points are called "quartiles", because they divide the data into quarters: one quarter of the data points are below the first quartile, one quarter between the first and second quartile (the median), and so on.)

The interquartile range is useful to get a rough idea of the spread of the data. The median by itself shows where the data are centered (or rather, shows one measure of central tendency); the interquartile range gives a better idea of how much the data points vary from this center.

Standard deviation

The standard deviation of a data set is a measurement of how much the data points vary from the mean. More precisely, it is equal to the square root of the average of the squares of the differences between each point and the mean: $s_x = \sqrt{\frac{\Sigma(X-\bar{X})^2}{N-1}}$.

The standard deviation is useful for determining the spread, or dispersion, of the data, or how far they vary from the mean. The smaller the standard deviation, the closer the values tend to be to the mean; the larger the standard deviation, the more they tend to be scattered far from the mean.

Outlier

An outlier is an extremely high or extremely low value in the data set. It may be the result of measurement error, in which case, the outlier is not a valid member of the data set. However, it may also be a valid member of the distribution. Unless a measurement error is identified, the experimenter cannot know for certain if an outlier is or is not a member of the distribution. There are arbitrary methods that can be employed to designate an extreme value as an outlier. One method designates an outlier (or possible outlier) to be any value less than $Q_1 - 1.5(IQR)$ or any value greater than $Q_3 + 1.5(IQR)$, where Q_1 and Q_3 are the first and third quartiles and IQR is the interquartile range. For instance, in the data set {42, 71, 22, 500, 33, 38, 62, 44, 58, 37, 61, 25}, the point 500 may be considered an outlier, since 500 is greater than 101.25 (61.5 + 1.5(26.5) = 101.25).

Regarding measurements of the center, outliers tend to have little or no effect on the mode, and in general little effect on the median, though their effects may be magnified for very small distributions. Means, however, are very sensitive to outliers; a single data point that lies far outside the range of the others may leave the mode and median almost unchanged while drastically altering the mean. For instance, the data set {2, 2, 5, 5, 5, 8, 11} has a mode and median of 5 and a mean of approximately 5.4; adding the outlying value 650 to the data set leaves the mode and median unchanged but increases the mean to 86. Like the median, the interquartile range is little affected by outliers, though, again, the effect may be greater for small data sets. The standard deviation, like the mean, is much more sensitive to outliers, and may be significantly increased by a single outlier that lies far from the spread of the rest of the points.

Shape of a measurement and its measures of central tendency

The measurement of central tendency with the most clearly visible relationship to the shape is the mode. The mode defines the peak of the distribution, and a distribution with multiple modes has multiple peaks. The relationship of the shape to the other measurements of central tendency is more subtle. For a symmetrical distribution with a single peak, the mode, median, and mean all coincide. For a distribution skewed to the left or right, however, this is not generally the case. One rule of thumb often given is that the median is displaced from the mode in the same direction as the skew of the graph, and the mean in the same direction farther still.

Two data sets with the same center but different spreads

It's certainly possible for two data sets to have the same center but different spreads; all that's necessary is for the points in one set to be clustered closer to the center than the other. Consider, for instance, two data sets that both have the normal distribution with the same mean but different standard deviations: all usual measurements of central tendency would match—the mean, mode, and median—but their spread, as measured by either interquartile range or by standard deviation, would differ. The graph below shows the distributions of two such data sets:

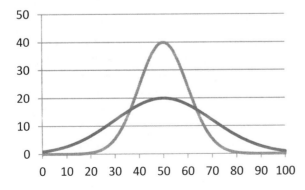

Two data sets with the same spread but different centers

It's certainly possible for two data sets to have the same spread but different centers; nothing prevents the data points of two sets from being equally near the center even if the center differs. Consider, for instance, two data sets that both have the normal distribution with the same standard deviation but different means: their spread, as measured by either interquartile range or by standard deviation, would match, but the measures of central tendency, mean, mode, and median—would differ between the data sets. The graph below shows the distributions of two such data sets:

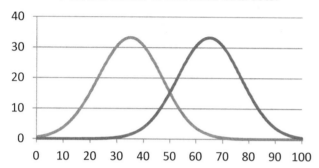

Two data distributions with the same spread and center but different shapes

It's certainly possible for two data distributions to have the same spread and center but different shapes. While the spread and the center are significant characteristics of a distribution, they are not sufficient to uniquely determine the distribution; two distributions may very well have the same spread and center but differ in the details. Consider, for instance, the data sets {5, 10, 15, 20, 25, 30, 35} and {7, 10, 11, 20, 29, 30, 33}: both these data sets have a mean and median of 20, an interquartile range of 20, and a standard deviation of approximately 10.8; yet clearly they are not identical, and have different shapes. For another example, consider an asymmetric distribution reflected about its mean; despite their different shapes, the distribution and its reflection have the same mean and necessarily the same spread.

Normal distribution

A normal distribution is a symmetrical, bell-shaped distribution that can be used to model real-world situations. In particular, the normal distribution is a good match for data that represents the sum or the mean of a large number of similar variables acting independently. If you roll a large number of dice, for instance, their mean will tend to follow close to a normal distribution.

The normal distribution has a number of useful properties. Perhaps the most notable is that the distribution of the sum or difference of two variables each of which follows the normal distributions is itself another normal distribution, with the mean equal to the sum or difference of the means of the distributions of the original variables, and the standard deviation equal to the square root of the sum of the squares of the standard deviations of the original distributions.

Fitting data to a normal distribution

The normal distribution is defined by the normal equation, $f(x) = \frac{1}{\sigma\sqrt{2\pi}}e^{-\frac{1}{2}\left(\frac{x-\mu}{\sigma}\right)^2}$, where μ is the mean and σ is the standard deviation. Generating a normal equation corresponding to a given mean and standard deviation, then, is as simple as putting the appropriate values for μ and σ into this equation. A standard deviation with a mean of 100 and a standard deviation of 10, for instance, would have a normal equation $f(x) = \frac{1}{10\sqrt{2\pi}}e^{-\frac{1}{2}\left(\frac{x-100}{10}\right)^2}$. The probability that the data lies within a certain range can be found by determining the area under the normal curve—the graph of the normal function—within the given range. It's often simpler, however, to consider the *standard normal distribution*, with the equation $f(z) = \frac{1}{\sqrt{2\pi}}e^{-\frac{1}{2}z^2}$. This is simply a normal distribution with a mean of 0 and a standard deviation of 1. A standard z-distribution is represented by the formula, $z = \frac{X-\mu}{\sigma}$.

Many data sets that arise in real-world problems can be fit to or at least approximated by a normal distribution, and given the useful properties of this distribution it's often useful to do so. However, the normal distribution is not a good fit for all data sets. In general, if a data set seems to follow a symmetrical bell curve, it is likely (though not necessarily the case) that it can be usefully fit to a normal distribution. For a data sets that is clearly skewed and asymmetrical, however, such a fit is not suitable. Nor is it appropriate to try to fit to a normal distribution data sets that have no peaks, or multiple peaks (though it may be possible to fit such data to a *sum* of normal distributions).

Estimating population percentages in a normal distribution

The population percentages falling within certain ranges in a normal distribution can be estimated by finding the area under the normal curve. This can either be estimated by inspection or determined using a calculator. For certain values, however, the population percentages can be estimated more directly. About 68% of the data points in a normal distribution lie within one standard deviation of the mean, about 95% within two standard deviations, and about 99.9% within three. For a normal distribution with a mean of 100 and a standard deviation of 10, for instance, we would expect 68% of the data points to lie between 90 and 110 (100 ± 10), and 95% of the data points to lie between 80 and 120. Because of the normal distribution's symmetry, half of these would lie on each side of the mean, so, for instance, about 34% of the data points would lie between 90 and 100 and 34% between 100 and 110; about 2.5% of the data points (½(100% – 95%)) would exceed 120.

Estimating the area under a normal curve

Calculator
Most scientific calculators have statistical functions that allow the easy calculation of probabilities related to common probability distributions, including the normal distribution. The details depend on the particular model of calculator. In the TI-84, one of the most commonly used calculators today, the appropriate function can be accessed from the DISTR button (press "2nd", and then "VARS"). This will bring up a menu of distribution-related functions; select "normalcdf". The parameters of this function are, in order, the lower bound, the upper bound, the mean, and the standard deviation. For a normal distribution with a mean of 100 and a standard deviation of 10, for instance, to find the

- 91 -

probability that a data point lies between 105 and 115 you would enter "normalcdf(105, 115, 100, 10)", yielding an answer of about 0.242, or 24.2%. If you desire to see the area visually, you can hit the right arrow from the DISTR menu to get to the DRAW menu, and choose "ShadeNorm". The parameters are the same as for the "normalcdf" function.

Spreadsheet

Most modern spreadsheet programs include functions that allow the user to find the area under a normal curve. In Microsoft Excel, the appropriate function is NORMDIST, which gives the total area of the graph to the left of a particular value. The first parameter of this function is the value in question, the second is the mean, and the third the standard deviation. The fourth parameter should be simply set to TRUE. (If it's set to FALSE, Excel will return the value of the normal function at that point rather than the area under the curve.) For instance, for a normal distribution with a mean of 100 and a standard deviation of 10, to find the area under the curve to the left of 115, you would enter into the cell "=NORMDIST(115,100,10,TRUE)".

To find the area within a given interval, you can simply take the difference of two results. For instance, for the previous example, the area of the curve between 105 and 115 would be generated by "=NORMDIST(115,100,10,TRUE)-NORMDIST(105,100,10,TRUE)".

Table

Z-tables are available and give the total area under a normal curve to the left of a given value (or the larger portion). The area within an interval can be found by taking the difference between the areas for the right and left endpoints. A mean to z table is also available and may be used to find the area between the mean and a given value. This table may also be used, in order to find the area to the left (or right) or a value, by adding half the area under the normal curve (0.5), to the mean to z area represented by the given value. Z-tables represent standardized values. The raw values are not represented by the table. Instead, the table represents standardized z-scores. A z-score is written as: $z = \frac{X-\mu}{\sigma}$, where X represents the particular value, μ represents the population mean, and σ represents the population standard deviation. (Literally translated, a z-score represents the number of standard deviations a value is above, or below, the mean.)For instance, if we wanted to find the area under the curve between 105 and 115 for a normal distribution with a mean of 100 and a standard deviation of 10, we would first convert our values to those appropriate for a normal distribution, $\frac{105-100}{10} = 0.5$ and $\frac{115-100}{10} = 1.5$, and then look up 1.5 and 0.5 in the table and subtract the results.

Two-way frequency table

A two-way frequency table is a table that shows the number of data points falling into each combination of two categories in the form of a table, with one category on each axis. Creating a two-way frequency table is simply a matter of drawing a table with each axis labeled with the possibilities for the corresponding category, and then filling in the numbers in the appropriate cells. For instance, suppose you're told that at a given school, 30 male students take Spanish, 20 take French, and 25 German, while 26 female students take Spanish, 28 French, and 21 German. These data can be represented by the following two-way frequency table:

# of students	SPANISH	FRENCH	GERMAN
MALE	30	20	25
FEMALE	26	28	21

Joint and marginal frequencies

The joint frequency, $P(X, Y)$, is the probability of belonging to two specific subcategories. It's also known as a joint probability or joint relative frequency. The marginal frequency, $P(X)$, is the probability of belonging in a specific subcategory. It's also known as a marginal probability or marginal relative frequency. For example,

		Category #1 (Color)			TOTALS
		yellow	grey	black	
Category #2 (Vehicle)	truck	2	5	20	27
	car	2	25	3	30
	motorcycle	15	4	3	22
TOTALS		19	34	26	79

The joint frequency that a vehicle is a yellow truck is equal to $\frac{2}{79}$, where 2 is the number in the table cell corresponding to both "truck" and "yellow" and 79 is the total number of all vehicles of all colors.

The marginal frequency that a vehicle is a truck is equal to the sum of the probabilities of its being a yellow truck, a grey truck, or a black truck, $P(truck) = \frac{2}{79} + \frac{5}{79} + \frac{20}{79} = \frac{27}{79}$.

Conditional frequency

The conditional frequency, P(X|Y), is the probability that X is a certain value on the condition that Y is a certain value. It's also known as a conditional probability or conditional relative frequency. The conditional frequency is related to the joint frequency and the marginal frequency by the relation $P(X, Y) = P(X|Y)P(Y)$; thus knowing the joint and marginal frequencies we can find the conditional frequency.
For example, consider the two-way frequency table below.

| | | Category #1 (Color) | | | TOTALS |
		yellow	grey	black	
Category #2 (Vehicle)	truck	2	5	20	27
	car	2	25	3	30
	motorcycle	15	4	3	22
TOTALS		19	34	26	79

The joint frequency that a vehicle is a yellow truck is equal to $\frac{2}{79}$, and the marginal frequency that a vehicle is a truck is $\frac{27}{79}$. Therefore, the conditional frequency that a vehicle is yellow on the condition that it is a truck (the probability that a given truck in the data set is yellow) is equal to $\frac{2}{79} \div \frac{27}{79} = \frac{2}{27}$.

Data on two quantitative variables on a scatter plot

Data sets on two quantitative variables can be represented on a scatter plot by plotting each data point as a separate point on the chart. One axis of the chart corresponds to each variable, and then the data points are plotted accordingly in the appropriate positions on each axis. For instance, if 50 widgets cost $500, 100 widgets cost $800, and 200 widgets cost $1500, this can be plotted on a scatter plot as follows:

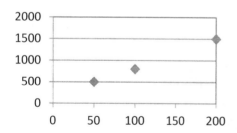

Normally, of course, a scatter plot would be used for larger data sets than this. A scatter plot is useful for seeing the relationship between the variables; one can often see at a glance if the variables have a linear or other simple relationship.

Identifying a function from a scatter plot of data of two variables

It's often possible from examining a scatter plot to see roughly what relationship exists between the data by estimating what kind of smooth curve would best fit the data points. Linear relationships are particularly easy to spot—do the data points look like they're roughly arranged in a straight line?—but other functions may also fit the data. Actually finding the parameters of the function for the most precise fit is a more complex matter, though most calculators and spreadsheets have the capability of performing the necessary calculations. Qualitatively judging what kind of function fits the data, however, is simpler. Below are examples of scatter plots fit to quadratic and exponential functions, respectively:

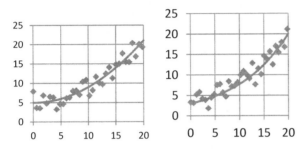

Using a function fitted to a scatter plot to solve problems

Linear functions
Once you have a function fitted to the scatter plot, you can use the equation of that function to solve problems regarding the data. For instance, suppose the scatter plot on the left below represents the number of bacteria that grow in a petri dish after one week, in millions, versus the amount of a certain nutrient added, in milligrams. The graph on the right shows a linear function fitted to the data.

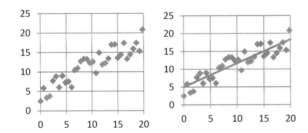

The equation of the line of best fit is $y = \frac{2}{3}x + 5$, where y is the bacteria count in millions and x is the amount of nutrient added, in milligrams. We can then use this function to solve problems; for instance, if we want to estimate how many bacteria to expect if we add 30 milligrams of nutrient, we solve $y = \frac{2}{3}(30) + 5 = 25$, or about 25 million bacteria.

Quadratic functions

Once you have a function fitted to the scatter plot, you can use the equation of that function to solve problems regarding the data. For instance, suppose the scatter plot on the left below represents the area covered by a certain patch of mold, in square centimeters, versus the time in days. The graph on the right shows a quadratic function fitted to the data.

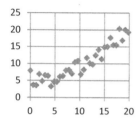 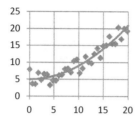

The equation of the quadratic trendline is $y = \frac{1}{25}x^2 + 5$, where x is the time in days and y is the area in square centimeters. We can then use this function to solve problems; for instance, if we want to estimate how much area to expect the mold to cover after 30 days, we solve $y = \frac{1}{25}(30^2) + 5 = 41$, or 41 square centimeters.

Exponential functions

Once you have a function fitted to the scatter plot, you can use the equation of that function to solve problems regarding the data. For instance, suppose the scatter plot on the left below represents the total assets of a certain company in millions of dollars, versus the time in years since 1990. The graph on the right shows an exponential function fitted to the data.

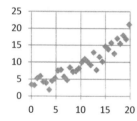 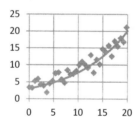

The equation of the trendline is $y = 3e^{0.095t}$, where t is the time in years and y is the company's assets, in millions of dollars. We can then use this function to solve problems; for instance, if we want to estimate the company's projected assets in the year 2020 (30 years after 1990), we solve $y = 3e^{0.095 \cdot 30} \approx 51.9$, or 51.9 million dollars.

Residuals of a fit to a data set

The residuals of a fit to a data set are the differences between the observed values of the data and the predicted values based on the fit. For example, consider the data set {(6,6), (8,12), (10,20), (12,30)}, shown in the scatter plot on the left below A linear fit to the graph is shown on the right:

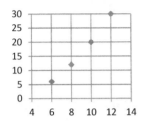 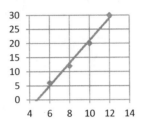

The line of best fit has the equation $y = 4x - 19$. The predicted value for $x = 6$ is then $4(6) - 19 = 5$, and the residual at $x = 6$ is $6 - 5 = 1$. At $x = 8$, the predicted value is $4(8) - 19 = 13$, and the residual at $x = 8$ is $12 - 13 = -1$. Similarly, the residuals at $x = 10$ and $x = 12$ are –1 and 1, respectively.

Note that these residuals add to 0 $(1 + (-1) + (-1) + 1 = 0)$. For the best fit curve, this is always the case; the sum and mean of the residuals will always be zero.

Residual plot

A residual plot is simply the plot of the residuals of a fit to a data set versus the independent variable (the x coordinates of the points). If the residual plot looks random—if the residuals seem to bear no relation to the independent variable—then the function fit to the model was probably a good choice. If the residual plot shows a definite pattern, then the data is probably better suited to a different kind of curve. Consider, for instance, the following two residual plots, both corresponding to linear fits. The plot on the left shows no obvious pattern, indicating that the linear fit in question is appropriate to the data. The plot on the left, however, shows a pronounced U shape, indicating that a nonlinear function would be a better fit to the data.

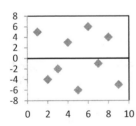 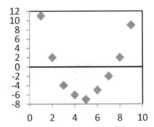

Estimating a fit to a linear function without the aid of technology

Although it's complicated to calculate an exact fit to a linear function without the aid of technology, finding an approximate fit is feasible. To produce such a fit, first draw a line that seems to follow the data points as closely as possible, probably with about as many data points above the line as below it. Then find the equation for this linear fit the same way as you would find the equation of any graphed line: choose two points on the line,

(x_1, y_1) and (x_2, y_2), and then find the slope of the line as $m = \frac{y_2 - y_1}{x_2 - x_1}$. Then use this value of m and one of the known points in the equation $y = mx + b$ to solve for b (it doesn't matter which of the two points you use).

Because this method involves some eyeballing and approximation, it will generally not be completely optimal, and two people may get slightly different results. However, this approximate result will typically be good enough to find estimated solutions to problems.

Finding a fit to a linear function using technology

Most modern calculators and spreadsheets have the functionality to calculate linear fits to data sets. On a TI-84, you can find the fit as follows: First, press "STAT", select "EDIT", and enter your data into the table, with the independent variable in the L1 column and the dependent in the L2. Then press "STAT" again, select "CALC", and select "LinReg(ax+b)". The screen will display the coefficients a and b of the linear fit.

In recent versions of Microsoft Excel, you can put the independent and dependent variables in adjacent columns, select all the data, and insert a scatter plot. Then right-click on one of the data points of the graph and select "Add Trendline". Select "Linear", and be sure to check "Display Equation on chart" before clicking OK. The linear plot should be displayed on the graph, along with the corresponding equation of the line.

Slope of a linear model

In the case of a linear fit to a data set, of the form $y = mx + b$, the slope m corresponds to the rate of change of the dependent variable y with respect to the independent variable x. This can often be expressed in a form similar to "y per x". For instance, if the data represents the distance of an object from some point as a function of time, with the distance as y and the time as x, then the slope of the linear model represents the change in distance with respect to the corresponding change in time—i.e., the velocity. If the data represents the cost to produce various quantities of products, then the slope of the linear model is the change in the cost with respect to the quantity of products produced—i.e., the production cost per unit of product.

Intercept of a linear model

In the case of a linear fit to a data set, of the form $y = mx + b$, the intercept b corresponds to the value of the dependent variable y when the independent variable x is equal to zero. This often can be expressed as the "initial value" of the variable, or as its offset. For instance, if the data represents the distance of an object from some point as a function of time, with the distance as y and the time as x, then the intercept of the linear model represents the object's distance at time zero—i.e., its initial distance. If the data represents the cost to produce various quantities of products, then the intercept of the linear model is the cost when no units are being produced—in other words, the overhead cost involved in the production.

Correlation coefficient of a linear fit

The correlation coefficient of a linear fit is a number that expresses how closely the linear fit approximates the function. The coefficient is negative if the line of best fit has a negative slope—the dependent variable decreases as the independent variable increases, and positive if the best fit has a positive slope—the dependent variable increases as the independent variable increases. The linear fit is most closely correlated to the data if the correlation coefficient is equal to ±1; this means that all the data points lie exactly on the best fit line. If the correlation coefficient is equal to 0, then the data are completely uncorrelated; there is no relationship between the dependent and the independent variable. More often, the correlation coefficient is somewhere in between 0 and 1, indicating a fit that reveals some correlation between the variables.

Computation using technology

Most modern calculators and spreadsheets have the functionality to calculate the correlation coefficients of linear fits to data sets. On a TI-84, you can find the fit as follows: First, press "STAT", select "EDIT", and enter your data into the table, with the independent variable in the L1 column and the dependent in the L2. Then press "STAT" again, select "CALC", and select "LinReg(ax+b)". In addition to the coefficients a and b of the linear fit, the screen will display the correlation coefficient, r.

In recent versions of Microsoft Excel, you can put the independent and dependent variables in adjacent columns, then in another cell type "=CORREL(". Select the cells containing the independent variables, then type a comma, select the cells containing the dependent variables and type a closing parenthesis. The cell should contain something like "=CORREL(A1:A10,B1:B10)", though the letters and numbers may differ. Press ENTER, and the cell will show the correlation coefficient of a linear fit to the data.

Two correlated variables

Two variables are correlated if some nonrandom relationship exists between them: if a change in one variable tends to correspond to a change in the other. While many relationships may exist between variables—they may have a quadratic relationship, or an exponential, for example—"correlation" often refers to linear correlation, the existence of a linear relationship $y = mx + b$ between the variables. The data points need not perfectly follow that line; if they do, they are perfectly correlated, but data that approximately follow close to a line may still be said to be correlated. The degree of correlation may be quantified by a value called the correlation coefficient.

Note that correlation is not the same thing as causation; just because two variables are correlated does not necessarily mean that one is the cause of the other.

Correlation and causation

Two variables are correlated if a change in one variable is accompanied by a change in the other, especially if the two variables have a linear relationship. Causation exists if one variable directly depends on the other; a change in one variable causes a change in the other. Note that correlation does not imply causation. If two variables x and y are correlated, it could be because x causes y. However, it could also be that the apparent correlation is coincidental, or that y causes x, or it could be that both x and y are influenced by a third variable separate from both *x* and *y*.

Two variables correlated but not linked by causation

Many examples could be constructed of data sets with variables that are correlated but in which one variable is not the cause of the other. One way to construct such a data set is to consider two variables that might both be affected by a third. For example, suppose a survey at a given school indicates that students' shoe sizes are correlated with their spelling; the students with larger shoe sizes tend to have better spelling. Clearly it would seem strange that larger feet would lead to better spelling. In fact, there's a third variable at play here: older students would tend to have larger feet, and likewise older students will tend to have better spelling. The larger shoe sizes don't cause the better spelling, nor does the better spelling cause the larger shoe sizes; rather, both are caused by a third variable that wasn't measured.

Practice Test #1

Practice Questions

1. $f(x) = 5x + 10$. If $x = 10$, then what is the value of $f(x)$?

   Ⓐ 25

   Ⓑ 60

   Ⓒ 12

   Ⓓ 5

2. The table below lists values for x and $f(x)$.

x	$f(x)$
1	2
2	5
3	10
4	17
5	26

   Which of the following equations describes the relationship between x and $f(x)$?

   Ⓐ $f(x) = x + 1$

   Ⓑ $f(x) = x^2$

   Ⓒ $f(x) = (-x)^2$

   Ⓓ $f(x) = x^2 + 1$

3. Mrs. Rose has 16 students in her class. Her class has three times as many girls as boys. How many girls and boys are in Mrs. Rose's class?

   Ⓐ 12 girls, 4 boys

   Ⓑ 4 girls, 12 boys

   Ⓒ 3 girls, 1 boy

   Ⓓ 9 girls, 7 boys

Questions 4 – 8 pertain to the following bar graph:

Liz set a goal to lose 30 pounds in 12 months. The figure below contains a bar graph that describes her weight in months 1 – 12.

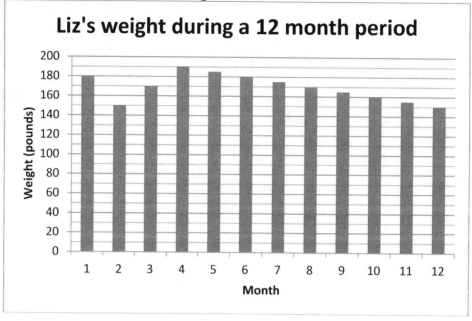

Figure: Bar graph for questions 4 – 8

4. What was Liz's initial weight?

Ⓐ 150 pounds

Ⓑ 170 pounds

Ⓒ 180 pounds

Ⓓ 195 pounds

5. How much weight did Liz lose by month 2?

Ⓐ 30 pounds

Ⓑ 20 pounds

Ⓒ 10 pounds

Ⓓ 0 pounds

6. Did Liz lose or gain weight from month 2 to month 4? How much weight did Liz lose or gain?

Ⓐ Liz lost 40 pounds

Ⓑ Liz gained 40 pounds

Ⓒ Liz lost 20 pounds

Ⓓ Liz gained 20 pounds

7. Which of the following statements is *not* supported by the weight loss data in Figure 1?

Ⓐ Liz lost 30 pounds by the second month of her diet.

Ⓑ Liz weighed more after the fourth month of her diet than she weighed at the beginning of her diet.

Ⓒ Liz experienced slow but consistent weight loss after month 4 of her diet.

Ⓓ Liz's rapid weight loss was sustainable for all 12 months of her diet.

8. Which of the following statements is most supported by the weight loss data in Figure 1?

Ⓐ The most Liz weighed was 180 pounds over the entire course of her diet

Ⓑ Liz lost weight every month during the entire 12 months of her diet

Ⓒ Liz did not meet her weight loss goal

Ⓓ Liz met her weight loss goal in month 12 through slow, consistent weight loss over time

9. Which of the following figures contains a graph of the function $y = 2x + 2$?

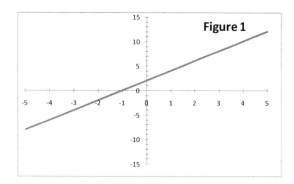

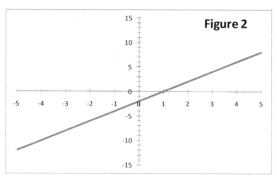

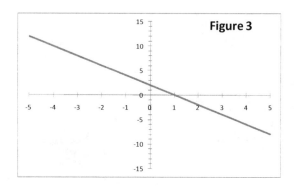

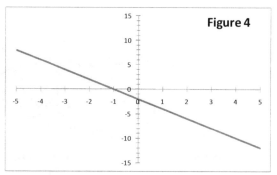

Ⓐ Figure 1

Ⓑ Figure 2

Ⓒ Figure 3

Ⓓ Figure 43

10. Which of the following figures contains a graph of the function $y = x^2 + 10$?

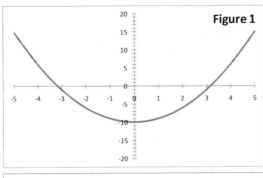

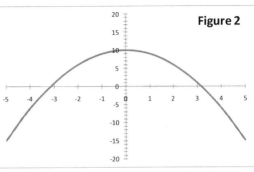

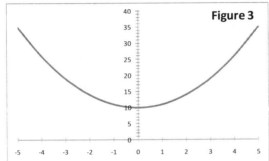

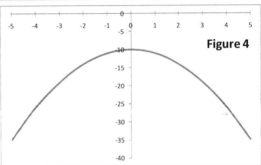

Ⓐ Figure 1

Ⓑ Figure 2

Ⓒ Figure 3

Ⓓ Figure 3

Questions 11 and 12 pertain to the following coordinate pairs:
$$\{(-5, 18), (-2, 12), (0, 3), (2,-3), (5,-12)\}$$

11. What is the domain of the coordinate pairs?

Ⓐ {18, 12, 3, -3, -12}

Ⓑ {-5, -2, 0, 2, 5}

Ⓒ {0, 3}

Ⓓ {-5, 18, 5, -12}

12. What is the range of the coordinate pairs?

Ⓐ {18, 12, 3, -3, -12}

Ⓑ {-5, -2, 0, 2, 5}

Ⓒ {0, 3}

Ⓓ {-5, 18, 5, -12}

Questions 13 and 14 pertain to the following scenario:

Aisha runs a small business selling candy bars to her classmates in school. She buys each candy bar for $0.75, and she sells each candy bar for $1.50. Let y represent Aisha's profit. Let x represent the number of candy bars she sells per day.

13. **Which equation best represents Aisha's daily profit from selling candy bars?**

Ⓐ $y = 0.75x - 1.50x$

Ⓑ $y = 0.75x + 0.75x$

Ⓒ $y = 1.50x + 0.75x$

Ⓓ $y = 1.50x - 0.75x$

14. **Which figure contains the graph that best represents Aisha's daily profit from selling candy bars?**

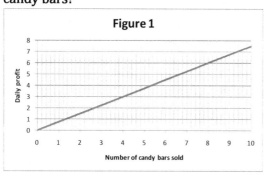

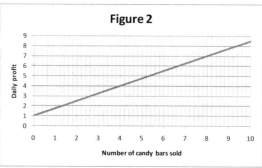

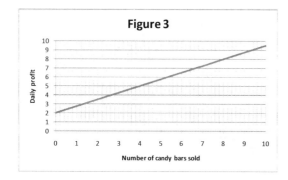

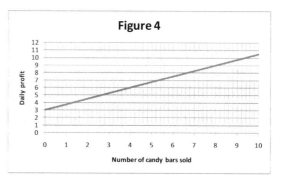

Ⓐ Figure 1

Ⓑ Figure 2

Ⓒ Figure 3

Ⓓ Figure 4

15. Consider two numbers, A and B. Let $A \Omega B = A2 + B2 - AB$. What is $2 \Omega 3$?

(A) 19

(B) 0

(C) 7

(D) -1

16. What are the factors of the following polynomial: $2x^2 + 7x - 15$?

(A) $(2x + 5)(x - 3)$

(B) $(x + 5)(2x - 3)$

(C) $(2x - 5)(x + 3)$

(D) $(x - 5)(2x + 3)$

17. What is the solution to the following equation: $x^2 - 9 = 0$?

(A) $x = 3$

(B) $x = -3$

(C) Both A and B are solutions to the equation

(D) Neither A nor B is a solution to the equation

18. What is the simplest form of the following polynomial?
$$4x^3 + x - x^3 + 2x^2 + 3 - 3x^3 + x - 2x^2 - 1$$

(A) $2x + 2$

(B) $x + 1$

(C) $x^3 + 1$

(D) $2(x + 1)$

19. Which of the following equations is an example of the distributive property?

(A) $(5)(3) = (3)(5)$

(B) $5 + 3 = 3 + 5$

(C) $(5)(1 + 2) = (5)(1) + (5)(2)$

(D) $15 = 15$

20. Which of the following equations is an example of the commutative property?

Ⓐ $(2)(7 + 8) = 14 + 16$

Ⓑ $14 + 16 = 16 + 14$

Ⓒ $(2)(7) + (2)(8) = (2)(15)$

Ⓓ $30 = 30$

Questions 21 – 25 pertain to the following chart:

John noticed that the number of points he scores during a basketball game is directly related to the number of hours he spends practicing each week. The table below lists John's weekly scores as a function of hours practiced. Let h represent the number of hours practiced and let p represent the number of points scored.

Number of hours practiced	Number of points scored during basketball game
2	11
4	21
6	31
8	41
10	51

21. Can the data presented in Table 2 be represented by a linear function?

Ⓐ Yes because the data can be written as a first-degree polynomial function of one variable.

Ⓑ Yes because the data can be written as a second-degree polynomial function of two variables.

Ⓒ No because the data cannot be written as a first-degree polynomial function of one variable.

Ⓓ No because the data cannot be written as a first-degree polynomial function of two variables.

22. Which equation represents the number of points John scored as a function of the number of hours he practiced?

Ⓐ $p(h) = 5h + 1$

Ⓑ $p(h) = 5h - 1$

Ⓒ $p(h) = p + 10$

Ⓓ $p(h) = p - 10$

23. If the number of points John scored during a basketball game were written as a linear function of the number of hours he practiced, which set of numbers below would represent the domain of that function?

Ⓐ {11, 21, 31, 41, 51}

Ⓑ {2, 4, 6, 8, 10}

Ⓒ {2, 11}

Ⓓ {10, 51}

24. If the number of points John scored during a basketball game were written as a linear function of the number of hours he practiced, which set of numbers below would represent the range of that function?

Ⓐ {11, 21, 31, 41, 51}

Ⓑ {2, 4, 6, 8, 10}

Ⓒ {2, 11}

Ⓓ {10, 51}

25. Which graph below best represents the relationship between the number of hours John practiced and number of points he scored?

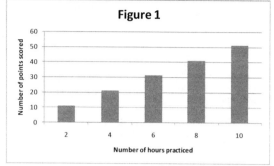

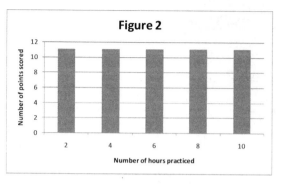

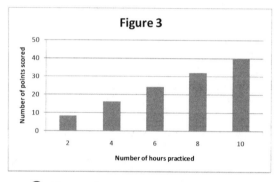

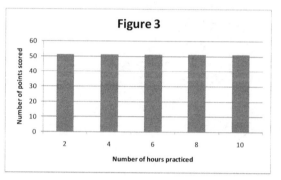

(A) Figure 1

(B) Figure 2

(C) Figure 3

(D) Figure 4

Questions 26 –28 pertain to the following graph:
The graph describes the change in distance over time for a particular car.

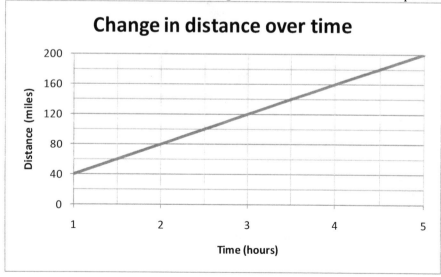

26. What is the slope of the line shown in the graph?

  Ⓐ 20

  Ⓑ 40

  Ⓒ 60

  Ⓓ 80

27. What are the units of the slope of the line?

  Ⓐ time per distance

  Ⓑ distance per time

  Ⓒ hours per miles

  Ⓓ miles per hour

28. What physical quantity does the slope measure? In other words, what does the slope tell you about the car's movement?

  Ⓐ The slope tells the car's speed

  Ⓑ The slope tells the total distance the car traveled

  Ⓒ The slope tells the total amount of time the car spent traveling

  Ⓓ The slope tells the amount of gas in the car

Questions 29 -31 pertain to the following Equation A:
  Let the equation of a line be described by Equation A: $5y - 100x = 25$

29. What are the slope and y-intercept of the line?

  Ⓐ The slope is 100, and the y-intercept is 5.

  Ⓑ The slope is 5, and the y-intercept is 100.

  Ⓒ The slope is 20, and the y-intercept is 5.

  Ⓓ the slope is 25, and the y-intercept is 5.

Question 30 pertains to the following information also:
  Suppose the equation of the same line is now described by Equation B:
  $5y - 200x = 75$

30. How does the slope of Equation B compare to the slope of Equation A?

Ⓐ The slope of Equation B is half the slope of Equation A

Ⓑ The slope of Equation B is twice the slope of Equation A

Ⓒ The slope of Equation B is 200 times the slope of Equation A

Ⓓ The slope of Equation B is the same as the slope of the Equation A

31. How does the y-intercept of Equation B compare to the y-intercept of Equation A?

Ⓐ The y-intercept of Equation B is twice the y-intercept of Equation A

Ⓑ The y-intercept of Equation B is three times the y-intercept of Equation A

Ⓒ The y-intercept of Equation B is 75 times the y-intercept of Equation A

Ⓓ The y-intercept of Equation B is the same as the y-intercept of Equation A

32. Line M contains the following two points: (1, 10) and (6, 20). What is the slope of line M?

Ⓐ 5

Ⓑ 2

Ⓒ 0.5

Ⓓ 10

33. Line Q has a slope of 10 and intercepts the y axis at point (0, -15). What is the equation of line Q?

Ⓐ $y = -15$

Ⓑ $y = -15x + 10$

Ⓒ $y = 15x - 10$

Ⓓ $y = 10x - 15$

34. The equation for line 1 is $y_x = 2x_1 + 6$ and the equation for line 2 is $y_2 = -x_2 - 3$. At what point does line 1 intersect line 2?

Ⓐ (-3, 6)

Ⓑ (6, -3)

Ⓒ (-3, 0)

Ⓓ (0,-3)

35. Table A below contains the x and y coordinates for several points on line P. Table B contains the x and y coordinates for several points on line Q. At what point does line P intersect line Q?

Table A: Coordinates for line P

x	y
-5	-8
-4	-4
-3	0
-2	4
-1	8
0	12
1	16

Table B: Coordinates for line Q

x	Y
-5	4
-4	2
-3	0
-2	-2
-1	-4
0	-6
1	-8

Ⓐ (-3, 0)

Ⓑ (-5, -8)

Ⓒ (0, -6)

Ⓓ (1, -8)

Questions 36 – 40 pertain to the following information:

Elli wants to plant a flower garden that contains only roses and tulips. However, she has a limited amount of space for the garden, and she can only afford to buy a specific number of each plant. Elli has enough space to plant a total of 20 flowers, and she has a total of $100 to purchase the flowers. Roses cost $14 per plant and tulips cost $4 per plant. Let R represent the number of roses and let T represent the number of tulips Elli will plant in her garden.

36. Which system of linear equations can be used to solve for the number of roses and tulips Elli will plant in her garden?

Ⓐ $\begin{cases} 4R + 14T = 20 \\ R + T = 100 \end{cases}$

Ⓑ $\begin{cases} R + T = 20 \\ 14R + 4T = 100 \end{cases}$

Ⓒ $\begin{cases} R + T = 20 \\ 4R + 14T = 100 \end{cases}$

Ⓓ $\begin{cases} 14R + 4T = 20 \\ 14R + 4T = 100 \end{cases}$

- 113 -

37. How many roses will Elli plant in her flower garden?

    Ⓐ 4

    Ⓑ 20

    Ⓒ 18

    Ⓓ 2

38. How many tulips will Elli plant in her flower garden?

    Ⓐ 4

    Ⓑ 20

    Ⓒ 18

    Ⓓ 2

39. Based on the information provided, why would Elli plant more tulips than roses in her garden?

    Ⓐ Because tulips require less space than roses

    Ⓑ Because tulips are less expensive than roses

    Ⓒ Because tulips are prettier than roses

    Ⓓ Because tulips require less fertilizer than roses

40. Suppose the local greenhouse has a sale, allowing Elli to purchase roses for $9 per plant. Now how many roses and tulips will Elli plant in her garden?

    Ⓐ 4 roses and 16 tulips

    Ⓑ 16 roses and 4 tulips

    Ⓒ 9 roses and 11 tulips

    Ⓓ 20 roses and 0 tulips

Questions 41 – 45 pertain to the following information:

    Joshua has to earn more than 92 points on the state test in order to qualify for an academic scholarship. Each question is worth 4 points, and the test has a total of 30 questions. Let x represent the number of test questions.

41. Which of the following inequalities can be solved to determine the number of questions Joshua must answer correctly?

Ⓐ $4x < 30$

Ⓑ $4x < 92$

Ⓒ $4x > 30$

Ⓓ $4x > 92$

42. How many questions must Joshua answer correctly?

Ⓐ $x < 30$

Ⓑ $x < 23$

Ⓒ $23 < x < 30$

Ⓓ $23 < x \leq 30$

43. Which of the following graphs best represents the number of questions Joshua must answer correctly?

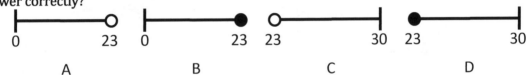

Ⓐ Graph A

Ⓑ Graph B

Ⓒ Graph C

Ⓓ Graph D

44. Let p represent the number of points. Which of the following inequalities best represents the number of points Joshua must earn on the state test?

Ⓐ $p < 30$

Ⓑ $p < 92$

Ⓒ $92 < p \leq 120$

Ⓓ $92 \leq p < 120$

45. Based on the information provided, if Joshua answers exactly 23 questions correctly, will he qualify for an academic scholarship?

Ⓐ Yes, because he will earn exactly 92 points for answering 23 questions correctly

Ⓑ Yes, because he will score higher than 75% for answering 23 questions correctly

Ⓒ No, because he must answer more than 23 questions correctly

Ⓓ No, because Joshua's parents earn too much money for him to qualify for a scholarship

Questions 46 – 49 pertain to the following information:
$$y_1 = x^2 \qquad y_2 = -x^2 \qquad y_3 = x^2 + 10$$

46. Which of the following numbers is included in the range of y_1?

Ⓐ 0

Ⓑ -1

Ⓒ -2

Ⓓ -3

47. How does function y_2 compare to the original function y_1?

Ⓐ y_2 has a different domain than y_1.

Ⓑ y_2 has a different range than y_1.

Ⓒ y_2 is shifted vertically by -1 unit when compared to y_1.

Ⓓ y_2 is shifted horizontally by -1 unit when compared to y_1.

48. How does function y_3 compare to the original function y_1?

Ⓐ y_3 is shifted vertically by +10 units when compared to y_1

Ⓑ y_3 is shifted vertically by -10 units when compared to y_1

Ⓒ y_3 is shifted horizontally by +10 units when compared to y_1

Ⓓ y_3 is shifted horizontally by -10 units when compared to y_1

49. Match the following graphs to their respective functions: y_1, y_2, and y_3.

Figure 1

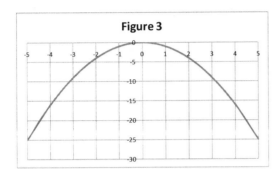

Figure 2

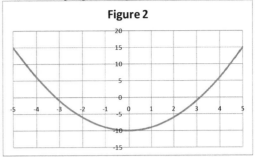

Figure 3

Figure 4

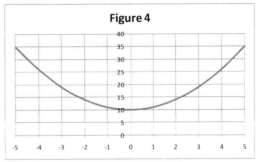

Ⓐ Figure 1 contains y_1. Figure 2 contains y_2. Figure 3 contains y_3

Ⓑ Figure 2 contains y_1. Figure 3 contains y_2. Figure 4 contains y_3

Ⓒ Figure 1 contains y_1. Figure 3 contains y_2. Figure 4 contains y_3

Ⓓ Figure 3 contains y_1. Figure 2 contains y_2. Figure 1 contains y_3

50. Solve the following equation for x, and write your answer in the answer grid.
$$x^2 + 10x = -25$$

-	0	0
+	1	1
	2	2
	3	3
	4	4
	5	5
	6	6
	7	7
	8	8
	9	9

51. At what value for x does the equation $x^2 + 10x = -25$ intercept the x-axis? Write your answer in the answer grid.

	-	0	0
	+	1	1
		2	2
		3	3
		4	4
		5	5
		6	6
		7	7
		8	8
		9	9

52. Consider the following equations:

$$x^2 = 4 \qquad x^3 = -8 \qquad x^4 = 16 \qquad x^5 = -32$$

What is x? Write your answer in the answer grid.

	-	0	0
	+	1	1
		2	2
		3	3
		4	4
		5	5
		6	6
		7	7
		8	8
		9	9

53. y is inversely proportional x such that $y = -\frac{1}{6}x$. If $y = 5$, what is x? Write your answer in the answer grid.

	-	0	0
	+	1	1
		2	2
		3	3
		4	4
		5	5
		6	6
		7	7
		8	8
		9	9

54. Solve the following equation for x:

$$2^x = 65536$$

Write your answer in the answer grid.

	-	0	0
	+	1	1
		2	2
		3	3
		4	4
		5	5
		6	6
		7	7
		8	8
		9	9

Answers and Explanations

1. B: The equation describes a functional relationship between x and $f(x)$. To solve the equation, substitute 10 as the value of x, such that $f(10) = 5(10) + 10 = 50 + 10 = 60$.

2. D: For each value of x, $f(x) = x^2 + 1$,
$$f(1) = (1)^2 + 1 = (1)(1) + 1 = 1 + 1 = 2$$
$$f(2) = (2)^2 + 1 = (2)(2) + 1 = 4 + 1 = 5$$
$$f(3) = (3)^2 + 1 = (3)(3) + 1 = 9 + 1 = 10$$
$$f(4) = (4)^2 + 1 = (4)(4) + 1 = 16 + 1 = 17$$
$$f(5) = (5)^2 + 1 = (5)(5) + 1 = 25 + 1 = 26$$

3. A: Let x represent the number of boys in Mrs. Rose's class. Since Mrs. Rose has three times as many girls in her class as boys, 3x represents the number of girls in Mrs. Rose's class. The total number of students in the class is 16. Written as an equation and solved for x we get:
$$x + 3x = 16$$
$$4x = 16$$
$$x = 4$$
Hence $x = 4$ and $3x = 12$. Therefore, 4 is the number of boys and 12 is the number of girls. Also,
$4 + 12 = 16$, the total number of students in the class.

4. C: According to the graph, in month 1, Liz weighed 180 pounds.

5. A: In month 1, Liz weighed 180 pounds. By month 2, Liz weighed 150 pounds. Since $180 - 150 = 30$, Liz lost 30 pounds by month 2.

6. B: In month 2, Liz weight 150 pounds but she weighed 190 pounds in month 4. Since $190 - 150 = 40$, Liz gained 40 pounds from month to month 4.

7. D: Liz experienced a rapid weight loss of 30 pounds by month 2; however she gained 40 pounds over the next 2 months, and her resulting weight was greater than her weight at the beginning of her diet. Therefore, her rapid weight loss was NOT sustainable for all 12 months of her diet.

8. D: Liz weighed 150 pounds by month 12, which was 30 pounds less than her initial 180 pounds. Thus Liz met her weight loss goal. Furthermore, from month 4 to month 12, Liz lost 5 pounds per month, which was means she met her goal through slow, consistent weight loss over time. Answer A is incorrect because Liz weight 190 pounds during month 4. Answer B is incorrect because Liz gained weight between month 2 and month 4. Answer C is incorrect because Liz did meet her 30 pound weight loss goal.

9. A: The equation is written in the form of the point slope formula: $y = mx + b$ where m is the slope of the line and b is the y-axis intercept. For the given equation $y = 2x + 2$, the slope of the line is positive 2 and the line intercepts the y-axis at positive 2. The graph in Figure 1 fits these criteria. The graph in Figure 2 intercepts the y-axis at negative 2. The graphs in Figure 3 and Figure 4 have slopes of negative 2.

10. C: The equation is written in the form $y = Ax^2 + B$ where A tells the concavity of the graph and B is the y- intercept. In this case, A equals positive 1. So the graph is concave up. B equals positive 10. So the graph intercepts the y-axis at positive 10. The graph in Figure 3 fits these criteria. The graph in Figure 1 intercepts the y-axis at negative 10. The graphs in Figure 2 and Figure 4 are concave down.

11. B: The list of coordinate pairs represents the x and y values of five points. The domain is all the x values. Answer B contains all the x values of the coordinate pairs.

12. A: The list of coordinate pairs represents the x and y values of five points. The range is all the y values. Answer A contains all the y values of the coordinate pairs.

13. D: To calculate Aisha's daily profit, first determine the amount of money Aisha earns from selling candy. Since x represents the number of candy bars she sells per day, and she sells each bar for $1.50, then her daily earnings equal 1.50x. Next, determine how much money Aisha spends buying the candy. Since each bar costs $0.75, she spends a total of 0.75x buying the candy. Finally, subtract the amount of money she spends buying the candy from the amount of money she earns selling the candy. Since y represents her daily profits, y = 1.50x – 0.75x.

14. A: The graph that represents Aisha's daily profit can be determined from the equation $y = 1.50x - 0.75x$. This equation can also be written as $y = (1.50 - 0.75)x$ or $y = 0.75x$. In its simplest form, the equation that describes Aisha's profits has a y-intercept of 0 and a slope of 0.75. The y-intercept tells the profits Aisha will earn if she sells no candy bars. Based on the equation, if Aisha sells no candy bars, then she earns no profit. The graph in Figure 1 fits these criteria.

15. C: Based on the definition of $A \Omega B$,
$$2 \, \Omega 3 = 2^2 + 3^2 - (2)(3)$$
$$= 4 + 9 - 6$$
$$= 13 - 6$$
$$= 7$$

16. B: To factor the polynomial, find factors of the first and third term whose product can be added to get the middle term. The fastest way to find the correct answer is to multiply the answer choices and select the choice that yields the original equation. In this case,
$$(x + 5)(2x - 3) = (x)(2x) + (x)(-3) + (5)(2x) + (5)(-3)$$
$$= 2x^2 - 3x + 10x - 15$$
$$= 2x^2 + 7x - 15$$

17. C: The solution to the equation follows:
$$x^2 - 9 = 0$$
$$x^2 = 9$$
$$x = \sqrt{9}$$
$$x = +3 \; and \; x = -3$$

18. D: To simplify the polynomial, group and combine all terms of the same order.
$$4x^3 + x - x^3 + 2x^2 + 3 - 3x^3 + x - 2x^2 - 1$$
$$= (4x^3 - x^3 - 3x^3) + (2x^2 - 2x^2) + (x + x) + (3 - 1)$$

$$= 0 + 0 + 2x + 2$$
$$= 2(x + 1)$$

19. C: The distributive property says that terms inside a set of parentheses can be multiplied by a factor outside the parentheses. In other words, $a(b + c) = ab + ac$. Answer C fits this definition.

20. B: A mathematical operation is commutative if altering the order does not alter the result of the operation. In other words, $a + b = b + a$ or $ab = ba$. Answer B fits this definition.

21. A: By definition, a linear function is a first degree polynomial function of one variable, and the data shown in Table 2 can be written as such. The variable is the number of hours practiced, and the score is a function of that variable.

22. A: In each case, the number of points scored p equals $5(h) + 1$ where h is the number of hours practiced. For example, $11 = (5)(2) + 1$ and $21 = (5)(4) + 1$. For answers C and D, the points scored are not written as functions of the hours practiced.

23. B: The domain consists of all the values of the independent variable. In this case, the independent variable is the number of hours practiced.

24. A: The range consists of all the values of the dependent variable. In this case, the depended variable is the number of points scored.

25. A: The bar graph shown in Figure 1 is the only graph where the number of points scored corresponds to the number of hours practiced as presented in Table 2.

26. B: The slope of a line describes the change in the dependent variable divided by the change in the independent variable, i.e. the change in y over the change in x. To calculate the slope, consider any two points on the line. Let the first point be $(1, 40)$, and let the second point be $(2, 80)$.
$$\frac{y_2 - y_1}{x_2 - x_1} = \frac{80 - 40}{2 - 1} = \frac{40}{1} = 40$$

27. D: The slope of the line is the change in y divided by the change in x. Therefore, the units of the slope are the units of y over the units for x. The unit for y is the unit for distance or miles. The unit for x is the unit for time or hours. Hence the units of the slope are miles over hour or miles per hour.

28. A: The slope describes the change in distance over the change in time. The change in distance over the change in time is a measure of the car's speed in miles per hour.

29. C: First write Equation A in slope-intercept form: $y = mx + b$ where m is the slope and b is the y-intercept.
$$5y - 100x = 25$$
$$5y = 100x + 25$$
$$y = 20x + 5$$

Based on the slope-intercept form of Equation A, the slope, m = 20 and the y-intercept, b = 5.

30. B: Write Equation B in slope-intercept form, which is $y = mx + b$:
$$5y - 200x = 75$$
$$5y = 200x + 75$$
$$y = 40x + 15$$
Based on the slope-intercept form of Equation B, the slope is 40, which is twice the slope of Equation A.

31. B: Based on the slope-intercept form of Equation B which is $y = mx + b$, the y-intercept is 15, which is three time the y-intercept of Equation A.

32. B: The slope of a line is the change in y divided by the change in x. Calculate the slope as follows:
$$m = \frac{y_2 - y_1}{x_2 - x_1} = \frac{20 - 10}{6 - 1} = \frac{10}{5} = 2$$

33. D: Write the equation in slope-intercept form: $y = mx + b$ where m is the slope of the line and b is the y-intercept. In this case, the slope m = 10 and the y-intercept b = -15. Hence $y = 10x - 15$.

34. C: At the intersection point of line 1 and line 2, $y_1 = y_2 = y$ and $x_1 = x_2 = x$. To find the x coordinate, let $y_1 = y_2$.
$$2x + 6 = -x - 3$$
$$2x + x = -6 - 3$$
$$3x = -9$$
$$x = -3$$
Now find the y coordinate by substituting x = -3 into either the equation for line 1 or the equation for line2.
$$y = 2x + 6$$
$$y = (2)(-3) + 6$$
$$y = -6 + 6$$
$$y = 0$$
Therefore, the point of intersection is (-3, 0).

35. A: The intersection point of line P and line Q will be common to both lines. See the explanation for question 34. Point (-3, 0) is the only point that is common to both lines.

36. B: Since Elli will plant a total of 20 flowers, the number of roses plus the number of tulips is 20 or $R + T = 20$. Each rose costs $14; so multiply the number of roses by 14. Each tulip costs $4; so multiply the number of tulips by 4. Elli has a total of $100 to spend on roses and tulips. So $14R + 4T = 100$.

37. D: Use a linear system of equations to find the number of roses. See the explanation for question 36. In this case, the system of equations is $R + T = 20$ and $14R + 4T = 100$. Begin with $R + T = 20$ and solve for T.
$$R + T = 20$$
$$T = 20 - R$$

Now substitute the equation for T into the equation $14R + 4T = 100$.

$$14R + 4T = 100$$
$$14R + 4(20 - R) = 100$$
$$14R + 80 - 4R = 100$$
$$10R = 20$$
$$R = 2$$

Therefore, Elli will plant 2 roses in her garden.

38. C: The number of roses, R is 2 and $R + T = 20$. Therefore, $T = 20 - 2 = 18$. Hence, Elli will plant 18 tulips in her garden.

39. B: Based on the given information, roses cost $14 while tulips cost only $4. Therefore, tulips are less expensive than roses. No information is given about the amount of space or fertilizer tulips require or about which flower Elli thinks is prettier.

40. A: The new price for roses requires defining a new system of equations. Elli will still plant a total of 20 flowers. Hence

$$R + T = 20$$
$$T = 20 - R$$

However, based on the new price for roses,

$$9R + 4T = 100$$
$$9R + 4(20 - R) = 100$$
$$9R + 80 - 4R = 100$$
$$5R = 20$$
$$R = 4$$

At the new price for roses, Elli will plant 4 roses in her garden. Since $R + T = 20$, Elli will plant 16 tulips in her garden.

41. D: In order to determine the number of questions Joshua must answer correctly, consider the number of points he must earn. Joshua will receive 4 points for each question he answers correctly, and x represents the number of questions. Therefore, Joshua will receive a total of 4x points for all the questions he answers correctly. Joshua must earn more than 92 points. Therefore, to determine the number of questions he must answer correctly, solve the inequality $4x > 92$.

42. D: See the explanation for question 41. To determine the number of questions Joshua must correctly answer, solve the following inequality:

$$4x > 92$$
$$x > \frac{92}{4}$$
$$x > 23$$

Therefore, Joshua must correctly answer at more than 23 questions to qualify for the scholarship. Because the test has a total of 30 questions, Joshua could answer all 30 questions correctly. Hence, the best inequality to describe the number of questions Joshua must correctly answer is $23 < x \leq 30$.

43. C: The inequality that best represents the number of questions Joshua must answer correctly is $23 < x \leq 30$. Hence, the left endpoint of the graph is 23, and the right endpoint is 30. Because Joshua must answer more than 23 questions, the endpoint at 23 is not included in the data set and is represented by an open circle.

44. C: According to the statement of the problem, Joshua must earn more than 92 points. Therefore, answers A and B are incorrect. Furthermore, answer D is incorrect because this answer says his score can equal 92 points but Joshua needs more than 92 points. Because the test has a total of 30 questions, and each question is worth 4 points, Joshua can earn a maximum of $(4)(30)$ or 120 points. Hence the best inequality is $92 < p \leq 120$.

45. C: Answers A and B are incorrect because Joshua must earn more than 92 points, which means he must correctly answer more than 23 questions. Answer D is incorrect because the problem statement mentions nothing about parental earnings.

46. A: The range is all the y values. Refer to a graph of y_1 shown below.

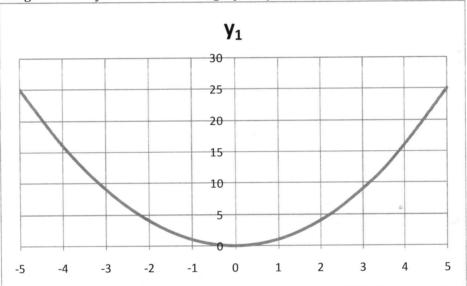

The minimum value for y is 0. Another way to solve this problem is to substitute the potential y values in the equation for y_1. For example,

$$y_1 = x^2$$
$$-1 = x^2$$
$$\sqrt{-1} = x$$

This statement has no real solution since it requires taking the square root of a negative number. Similar solutions are obtained if $y = -2$ or if $y = -3$.

47. B: The original function y_1 is concave up. See the graph of y_1 shown in the explanation for problem 46. Changing the coefficient of x^2 from +1 to -1 causes the function to be concave down. See the graph of y_2 shown below.

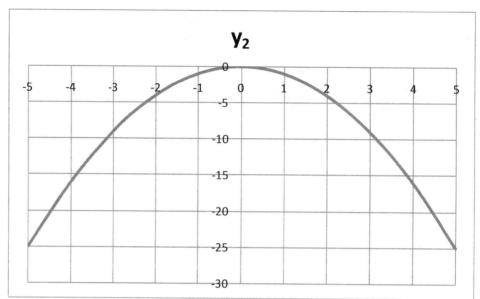

The y values for y_2 are different from those of y_1. Therefore, y_2 has a different range than y_1.

48. A: For function y_1, the y-intercept is 0. See the graph of y_1 shown in the explanation for problem 46. For function y_3, the y-intercept is +10. See the graph of y_3 shown below.

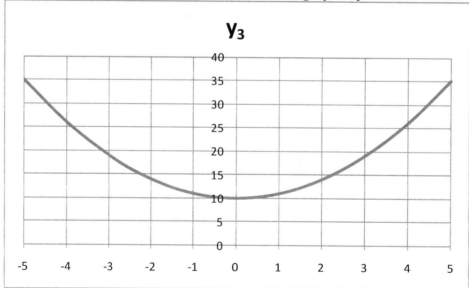

The graph of y_3 is similar to that of y_1 except the y-intercept of y_3 is 10 units above that of y_1. In other words, the difference between +10 and 0 is 10 units.

49. C: The graphs for y_1, y_2, and y_3 are displayed in the explanations for questions 46 – 48.

50. The correct answer is **x = -5**. The solution follows:
$$x^2 + 10x = -25$$
$$x^2 + 10x + 25 = 0$$
$$(x + 5)(x + 5) = 0$$
$$x = -5$$

51. The correct answer is **x = -5**. The x-intercept is determined by setting the equation equal to zero and then solving for x. When $x^2 + 10x + 25 = 0$, then x = -5.

52. The correct answer is **x = -2**. Because x² = 4, we can quickly determine that the magnitude of x is 2. The sign, however, alternates between positive and negative. Therefore, x must be -2. Note that multiplying a negative number by itself an even number of times yields a positive number. Multiplying a negative number by itself an odd number of times yields a negative number.

53. The correct answer is **x = -30**. The solution follows:
$$y = -\frac{1}{6}x$$
$$6y = -x$$
$$-6y = x$$
$$(-6)(5) = x$$
$$-30 = x$$

54. The correct answer is **x = 16**. The solution follows:
$$2^x = 65536$$
$$x\log2 = \log 65536$$
$$x = \frac{\log 65536}{\log 2}$$
$$x = 16$$

Practice Test #2

Practice Questions

1. $p(y) = \frac{4y}{2} + 5$. If $y = 4$, then what is the value of $p(y)$?

   Ⓐ 9

   Ⓑ 7

   Ⓒ 13

   Ⓓ 37

2. The table below lists values for y and p(y).

y	p(y)
1	2
-1	2
2	5
-2	5
3	10
-3	10

   Which of the following equations describes the relationship between y and p(y)?

   Ⓐ $p(y) = y + 1$

   Ⓑ $p(y) = 2y + 1$

   Ⓒ $p(y) = (y)^2$

   Ⓓ $p(y) = (y)^2 + 1$

3. Mr. Robinson has 20 students in his martial arts class. The ratio of boys to girls is 4:1. How many boys and girls are in Mr. Robinson's class?

   Ⓐ 15 boys, 5 girls

   Ⓑ 5 boys, 15 girls

   Ⓒ 16 boys, 4 girls

   Ⓓ 4 boys, 16 girls

Questions 4 – 6 pertain to the following passage:

Mrs. Langston owns an orchard with several different kinds of fruit trees. Half the trees are apple trees, one quarter are pear trees, approximately one eighth are orange trees and about one eighth are lemon trees.

4. Which of the pie graphs below best describes the percentage of trees in Mrs. Langston's orchard?

Ⓐ Figure A

Ⓑ Figure B

Ⓒ Figure C

Ⓓ Figure D

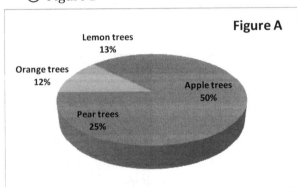

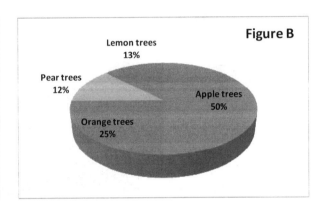

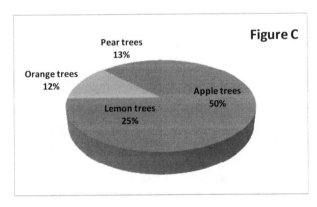

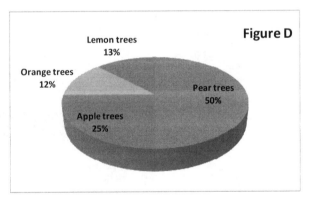

5. If Mrs. Langston has a total of 100 trees in her orchard, how many of each type of tree does she have?

Ⓐ 50 apple trees, 25 orange trees, 13 lemon trees, and 12 pear trees

Ⓑ 50 apple trees, 25 pear trees, 13 lemon trees, and 12 orange trees

Ⓒ 50 apple trees, 25 lemon trees, 13 pear trees, and 12 orange trees

Ⓓ 50 pear trees, 25 apple trees, 13 lemon trees, and 12 orange trees

6. Let y= the number of apple trees and let p(y) = the number of pear trees in Mrs. Langston's orchard. Which of the following equations best represents the relationship between apple trees and pear trees?

Ⓐ $p(y) = 2y$

Ⓑ $p(y) = \frac{y}{2}$

Ⓒ $p(y) = \frac{y}{4}$

Ⓓ $p(y) = \frac{y}{8}$

7. Based on the ratio of trees in Mrs. Langston's, she could probably produce the largest amount of which of the following products?

Ⓐ Lemonade

Ⓑ Orange juice

Ⓒ Apple sauce

Ⓓ Pear preserves

8. Based on the ratio of trees Mrs. Langston has in her orchard, which of the following statements is most likely false?

Ⓐ Mrs. Langston plants fewer lemon trees and orange trees because she earns the least amount of money from selling these fruits.

Ⓑ Mrs. Langston plants fewer pear trees than apple trees because pears are less profitable than apples.

Ⓒ Mrs. Langston plants more apple trees than any other kind of fruit because she earns the most money from selling apples.

Ⓓ Mrs. Langston plants more pear trees than any other kind of fruit because she earns the most money from selling pears.

9. Which of the following figures contains a graph of the function y = -3x – 3?

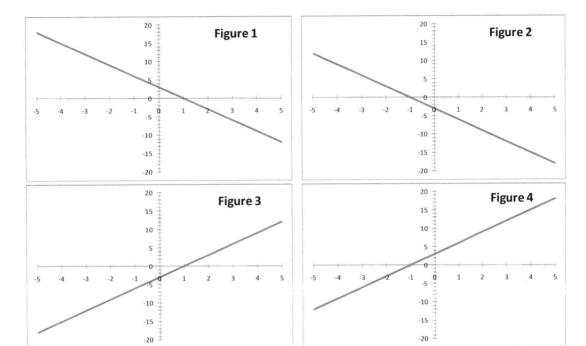

Ⓐ Figure 1

Ⓑ Figure 2

Ⓒ Figure 3

Ⓓ Figure 4

10. Which of the following figures contains a graph of the function $y = -x^2 - 5$?

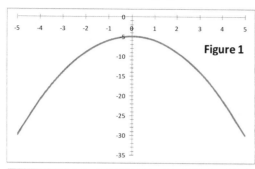

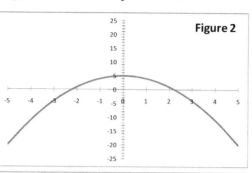

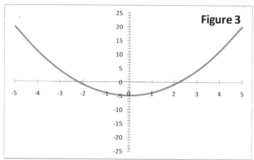

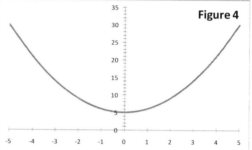

Ⓐ Figure 1

Ⓑ Figure 2

Ⓒ Figure 3

Ⓓ Figure 4

Questions 11 – 12 pertain to the following coordinate pairs:
{(5,8), (3,4), (-1,-4), (-3, -8), (-5,-12)}
11. What is the range of the coordinate pairs?

Ⓐ {5, 8, -5, -12}

Ⓑ {-1, -4}

Ⓒ {-5, -3, -1, 3, 5}

Ⓓ {-12, -8, -4, 4, 8}

12. What is the domain of the coordinate pairs?

Ⓐ {5, 8, -5, -12}

Ⓑ {-1, -4}

Ⓒ {-5, -3, -1, 3, 5}

Ⓓ {-12, -8, -4, 4, 8}

Questions 13 – 14 pertain to the following scenario:

During the summers, Tyrone earns money by mowing lawns in his neighborhood. For each lawn he mows, Tyrone charges $10 per hour plus a $10 fee to cover gas and maintenance for his lawn mower. Let y represent the money Tyrone earns from mowing a single lawn. Let x represent the number of hours Tyrone spends mowing a single lawn.

13. Which equation best represents the amount of money Tyrone earns from mowing a single lawn?

Ⓐ $y = 20x$

Ⓑ $y = 10x$

Ⓒ $y = 10x + 10$

Ⓓ $y = 10x - 10$

14. Which figure contains the graph that best represents Tyrone's earnings per lawn?

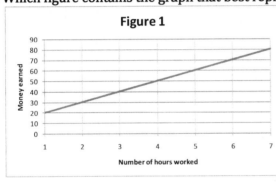

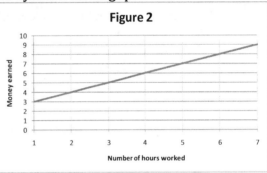

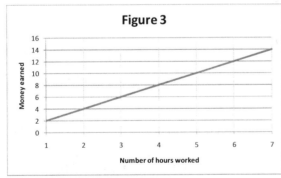

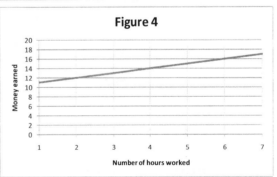

Ⓐ Figure 1

Ⓑ Figure 2

Ⓒ Figure 3

Ⓓ Figure 4

15. Consider two numbers, A and B. Let $A\theta B = 2A + 3B - A - B$. What is $1\theta 2$?

    Ⓐ 4

    Ⓑ 5

    Ⓒ 0

    Ⓓ 8

16. What are the factors of the following polynomial: $x^2 - x - 56$?

    Ⓐ $(x - 7)(x + 8)$

    Ⓑ $(x + 7)(x - 8)$

    Ⓒ $(x - 7)(x - 8)$

    Ⓓ $(x + 7)(x + 8)$

17. What is the solution to the following equation: $x^2 - 25 = 0$?

    Ⓐ $x = 5$

    Ⓑ $x = -5$

    Ⓒ Neither A nor B is a solution to the equation

    Ⓓ Both A and B are solutions to the equation

18. What is the simplest form of the following polynomial:
$$4x^3 + 5x - x^3 + 2x^2 + 17 - 3x^3 + 5x - 2x^2 + 3$$

    Ⓐ $10x + 20$

    Ⓑ $X + 2$

    Ⓒ $10(x + 2)$

    Ⓓ $4x^3 + 2$

19. Which of the following equations is an example of the commutative property?

    Ⓐ $(3)(6 + 10) = 18 + 30$

    Ⓑ $18 + 30 = 30 + 18$

    Ⓒ $(3)(6) + (3)(10) = 3(16)$

    Ⓓ $48 = 48$

20. Which of the following equations is an example of the distributive property?

  Ⓐ $(4)(2) = (2)(4)$

  Ⓑ $4 + 2 = 2 + 4$

  Ⓒ $(2)(1 + 3) = (2)(1) + (2)(3)$

  Ⓓ $8 = 8$

Questions 21 – 25 pertain to the following information:
    Gwendolyn noticed that the number of points she scores during a basketball game is directly related to the number of hours she spends practicing each week. The table below lists Gwendolyn's weekly scores as a function of hours practiced. Let h represent the number of hours practiced and let p represent the number of points scored.

Number of hours practiced	Number of points scored during basketball game
2	8
4	14
6	20
8	26
10	32

21. Can the data presented in Table 2 be represented by a linear function?

  Ⓐ Yes because the data can be written as a second-degree polynomial function of two variables.

  Ⓑ Yes because the data can be written as a first-degree polynomial function of one variable.

  Ⓒ No because the data cannot be written as a first-degree polynomial function of one variable.

  Ⓓ No because the data cannot be written as a first-degree polynomial function of two variables.

22. Which equation represents the number of points Gwendolyn scored as a function of the number of hours she practiced?

  Ⓐ $p(h) = 3h + 2$

  Ⓑ $p(h) = 3h - 2$

  Ⓒ $p(h) = p + 6$

  Ⓓ $p(h) = p - 6$

23. If the number of points Gwendolyn scored during a basketball game were written as a linear function of the number of hours she practiced, which set of numbers below would represent the range of that function?

Ⓐ {10, 32}

Ⓑ {2, 8}

Ⓒ {2, 4, 6, 8, 10}

Ⓓ {8, 14, 20, 26, 32}

24. If the number of points Gwendolyn scored during a basketball game were written as a linear function of the number of hours she practiced, which set of numbers below would represent the domain of that function?

Ⓐ {10, 32}

Ⓑ {2, 8}

Ⓒ {2, 4, 6, 8, 10}

Ⓓ {8, 14, 20, 26, 32}

25. Which graph below best represents the relationship between the number of hours Gwendolyn practiced and number of points she scored?

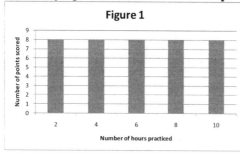

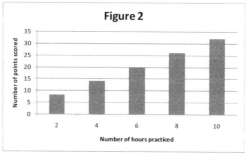

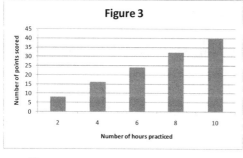

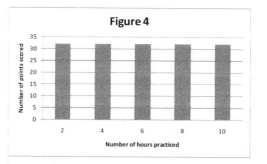

Ⓐ Figure 1

Ⓑ Figure 2

Ⓒ Figure 3

Ⓓ Figure 4

The following graph describes the change in distance over time for a cheetah hunting her prey. Use this graph to answer question 26 – question 28:

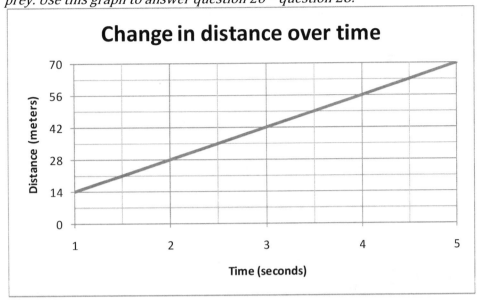

26. What is the slope of the line shown in the graph?

Ⓐ 28

Ⓑ 21

Ⓒ 14

Ⓓ 7

27. What are the units of the slope of the line?

Ⓐ seconds per meter

Ⓑ time per distance

Ⓒ meters per second

Ⓓ distance per time

28. What physical quantity does the slope measure? In other words, what does the slope tell you about the cheetah's movement?

Ⓐ The slope tells the cheetah's speed

Ⓑ The slope tells the total distance the cheetah traveled

Ⓒ The slope tells the total amount of time the cheetah spent chasing her prey

Ⓓ The slope tells how long the cheetah sleeps

Use Equation A to answer question 29 – question 31:

Let the equation of a line be described by Equation A:

$$10y - 5x = 40.$$

29. What are the y-intercept and slope of the line?

  Ⓐ The y-intercept is 40, and the slope is 10

  Ⓑ The y-intercept is 10, and the slope is 40

  Ⓒ The y-intercept is 40, and the slope is 2

  Ⓓ The y-intercept is 4, and the slope is 0.5

30. Suppose the equation of the same line is now described by Equation B:

$$10y - 10x = 20.$$

How does the slope of Equation B compare to the slope of Equation A?

  Ⓐ The slope of Equation B is twice the slope of Equation A.

  Ⓑ The slope of Equation B is the same as the slope of Equation A.

  Ⓒ The slope of Equation B is half the slope of Equation A.

  Ⓓ The slope of Equation B cannot be determined.

31. How does the y-intercept of Equation B compare to the y-intercept of Equation A?

  Ⓐ The y-intercept of Equation B is twice the y-intercept of Equation A

  Ⓑ The y-intercept of Equation B is the same as the y-intercept of Equation A

  Ⓒ The y-intercept of Equation B is half the y-intercept of Equation A

  Ⓓ The y-intercept of Equation B cannot be determined

32. Line W contains the following two points: (3, 30) and (8, 75). What is the slope of line W?

  Ⓐ 3

  Ⓑ 9

  Ⓒ 30

  Ⓓ 75

33. Line G has a slope of 20 and intercepts the y axis at point (0, 100). What is the equation of line G?

Ⓐ $y = 100$

Ⓑ $y = 20$

Ⓒ $y = 20x - 100$

Ⓓ $y = 20x + 100$

34. The equation for line 1 is $y_1 = 8x_1 - 16$ and the equation for line 2 is $y_2 = -4x_2 + 20$. At what point does line 1 intersect line 2?

Ⓐ $(3, 8)$

Ⓑ $(8, 3)$

Ⓒ $(-16, 20)$

Ⓓ $(20, -16)$

35. Table A below contains the x and y coordinates for several points on line P. Table B contains the x and y coordinates for several points on line Q. At what point does line P intersect line Q?

Table A: Coordinates for line P

x	y
5	56
1	24
-3	-8
-9	-56
-20	-144

Table B: Coordinates for line Q

x	Y
5	0
1	-16
-3	-32
-9	-56
-20	-100

Ⓐ $(-20, -100)$

Ⓑ $(-9, -56)$

Ⓒ $(1, 24)$

Ⓓ $(5, 56)$

Questions 36 – 40 pertain to the following information:

Vivian wants to plant a vegetable garden that contains only tomatoes and cucumbers. However, she has a limited amount of space for the garden, and she can only afford to buy a specific number of each vegetable. Vivian has enough space to plant a total of 40 vegetables, and she has a total of $80 to purchase the vegetables. Tomatoes cost $1 per plant and cucumbers cost $3 per plant. Let T represent the number of tomatoes and let C represent the number of cucumbers Vivian will plant in her garden.

36. Which system of linear equations can be used to solve for the number of tomatoes and cucumbers Vivian will plant in her garden?

Ⓐ $T + C = 40$ and $T + 3C = 80$

Ⓑ $T + 3C = 40$ and $T + C = 80$

Ⓒ $T + C = 80$ and $T + 3C = 40$

Ⓓ $3T + C = 80$ and $T + C = 40$

37. How many tomatoes will Vivian plant in her vegetable garden?

Ⓐ 10

Ⓑ 20

Ⓒ 30

Ⓓ 40

38. How many cucumbers will Vivian plant in her vegetable garden?

Ⓐ 10

Ⓑ 20

Ⓒ 30

Ⓓ 40

39. Based on the information provided, is it possible that Vivian will plant the same number of tomatoes as cucumbers?

Ⓐ No, because cucumbers cost 3 times as much as tomatoes

Ⓑ No, because cucumbers require more space than tomatoes

Ⓒ Yes, because Vivian has enough money to purchase the same amount of tomatoes and cucumbers, despite the price difference

Ⓓ Yes, because Vivian likes tomatoes and cucumbers equally

40. Suppose Vivian landscapes her yard, and now she has enough space to plant a total of 50 vegetables. How many tomatoes and cucumbers will Vivian plant in her garden?

Ⓐ 25 tomatoes and 25 cucumbers

Ⓑ 40 tomatoes and 10 cucumbers

Ⓒ 15 tomatoes and 35 cucumbers

Ⓓ 35 tomatoes and 15 cucumbers

Questions 41 – 45 pertain to the following information:
Matthew has to earn more than 96 points on his high school entrance exam in order to be eligible for varsity sports. Each question is worth 3 points, and the test has a total of 40 questions. Let x represent the number of test questions.

41. Which of the following inequalities can be solved to determine the number of questions Matthew must answer correctly?

Ⓐ $3x > 96$

Ⓑ $3x < 96$

Ⓒ $3x > 40$

Ⓓ $3x < 40$

42. How many questions can Matthew answer incorrectly and still qualify for varsity sports?

Ⓐ $x > 32$

Ⓑ $x > 8$

Ⓒ $0 \leq x < 8$

Ⓓ $0 < x \leq 8$

43. Which of the following graphs best represents the number of questions Matthew can answer incorrectly?

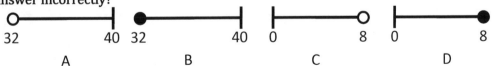

Ⓐ Graph A

Ⓑ Graph B

Ⓒ Graph C

Ⓓ Graph D

44. Let p represent the number of points. Which of the following inequalities best represents the number of points Matthew must earn on the entrance exam?

Ⓐ $96 \leq p < 120$

Ⓑ $96 < p \leq 120$

Ⓒ $p < 96$

Ⓓ $p < 32$

45. Based on the information provided, if Matthew answers exactly 32 questions correctly, will he qualify for varsity sports?

Ⓐ Yes, because he will earn exactly 96 points for answering 32 questions correctly

Ⓑ Yes, because he will score 80% for answering 32 questions correctly

Ⓒ No, because he must answer more than 32 questions correctly

Ⓓ No, because Matthew would rather get a part-time job than play varsity sports

Questions 46 – 49 pertain to the following information:
$$y_1 = 2x^2 + 3 \qquad y_2 = -2x^2 + 3 \qquad y_3 = 2x^2 - 3$$

46. Which of the following numbers is included in the range of y_1?

Ⓐ 0

Ⓑ 1

Ⓒ 2

Ⓓ 3

47. How does function y_2 compare to the original function y_1?

Ⓐ y_2 has a different domain than y_1

Ⓑ y_2 has a different range than y_1

Ⓒ y_2 is shifted vertically by -2 units when compared to y_1

Ⓓ y_2 is shifted horizontally by -2 units when compared to y_1

48. How does function y_3 compare to the original function y_1?

Ⓐ y_3 is shifted vertically by -3 units when compared to y_1

Ⓑ y_3 is shifted vertically by -6 units when compared to y_1

Ⓒ y_3 is shifted vertically by +3 units when compared to y_1

Ⓓ y_3 is shifted vertically by +6 units when compared to y_1

49. Match the following graphs to their respective functions: y_1, y_2, and y_3.

Figure 1

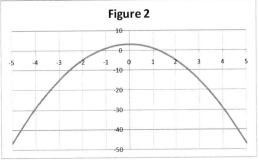

Figure 2

Figure 3

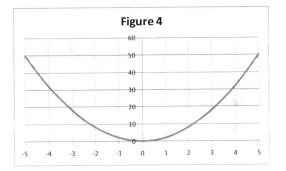

Figure 4

Ⓐ Figure 1 contains y_1. Figure 2 contains y_2. Figure 3 contains y_3

Ⓑ Figure 2 contains y_1. Figure 3 contains y_2. Figure 4 contains y_3

Ⓒ Figure 4 contains y_1. Figure 3 contains y_2. Figure 2 contains y_3

Ⓓ Figure 3 contains y_1. Figure 2 contains y_2. Figure 1 contains y_3

50. Solve the following equation for x, and write your answer in the answer grid.

$$x^2 + 4x = -4$$

-	0	0
+	1	1
	2	2
	3	3
	4	4
	5	5
	6	6
	7	7
	8	8
	9	9

51. At what value for x does the equation $x^2 + 4x = -4$ intercept the x-axis? Write your answer in the answer grid.

	0	0
-	0	0
+	1	1
	2	2
	3	3
	4	4
	5	5
	6	6
	7	7
	8	8
	9	9

52. Consider the following equations:

$$x^2 = 1 \qquad x^3 = -1 \qquad x^4 = 1 \qquad x^5 = -1$$

What is x? Write your answer in the answer grid.

	0	0
-	0	0
+	1	1
	2	2
	3	3
	4	4
	5	5
	6	6
	7	7
	8	8
	9	9

53. y is inversely proportional to x such that $y = -\frac{1}{3}x$. If $y = 9$, what is x? Write your answer in the answer grid.

	0	0
-	0	0
+	1	1
	2	2
	3	3
	4	4
	5	5
	6	6
	7	7
	8	8
	9	9

54. Solve the following equation for x:

$$2^x = 4096$$

Write your answer in the answer grid.

-	0	0
+	1	1
	2	2
	3	3
	4	4
	5	5
	6	6
	7	7
	8	8
	9	9

Answers and Explanations

1. C: The equation describes a functional relationship between y and p(y). To solve the equation, substitute 4 as the value of y, such that

$$p(4) = \frac{4(4)}{2} + 5 = \frac{16}{2} + 5 = 8 + 5 = 13.$$

2. D: For each value of y, $p(y) = (y)^2 + 1$

$$p(1) = (1)^2 + 1 = (1)(1) + 1 = 1 + 1 = 2$$
$$p(-1) = (-1)^2 + 1 = (-1)(-1) + 1 = 1 + 1 = 2$$
$$p(2) = (2)^2 + 1 = (2)(2) + 1 = 4 + 1 = 5$$
$$p(-2) = (-2)^2 + 1 = (-2)(-2) + 1 = 4 + 1 = 5$$
$$p(3) = (3)^2 + 1 = (3)(3) + 1 = 9 + 1 = 10$$
$$p(-3) = (-3)^2 + 1 = (-3)(-3) + 1 = 9 + 1 = 10$$

3. C: Let y = the number of girls in Mr. Robinson's class. The ratio of boys to girls is 4:1. So for every 1 girl in the class, there are 4 boys in the class. Therefore, $4y$ equals the number of boys in Mr. Robinson's class. The total number of students in the class is 20. Therefore, the number of boys plus the number of girls equals 20 or

$$y + 4y = 20$$
$$5y = 20$$
$$y = 4$$

Hence y = 4 and 4y = 16. Therefore, 4 = the number of girls and 16 = the number of boys. Also, 4 + 16 = 20, the total number of students in the class.

4. A: Since half of the orchard contains apple trees, apple trees = 50%. In other words, $\frac{1}{2} = 0.5 = 50\%$. One quarter of the orchard contains pear trees. So pear trees = 25% or $\frac{1}{4} = 0.25 = 25\%$. Approximately one eighth of the orchard contains orange trees and one eighth contains lemon trees. One eighth is 12.5%, rounded to nearest whole number gives orange trees = 12% and lemon trees = 13%.

5. B: We know that apple trees = 50%, pear trees = 25%, lemon trees = 13%, and orange trees = 12%. Each percentage represents a portion of the total 100%. If the total number of trees is 100, then
apple trees = (50%) (100) = (0.5)(100) = 50 trees,
pear trees = (25%)(100) = (0.25)(100) = 25 trees,
lemon trees = (13%)(100) = (0.13)(100) = 13 trees,
orange trees = (12%)(100) = (0.12)(100) = 12 trees

6. B: Let y represent the number of apple trees. Then $p(y)$ represents the number of pear trees as a function of apple trees. Since Mrs. Langston has half as many pear trees as apple trees, the relationship can be represented as $(y) = \frac{1}{2}y = \frac{y}{2}$.

7. C: Mrs. Langston has more apples in her orchard than any other fruit. Therefore, she could most likely produce the largest amount of a product that comes from apples, which in this case, is apple sauce.

8. D: The statement is false because Mrs. Langston did not plant more pear trees than any other kind of fruit. Instead, she planted the most *apple* trees.

9. B: The equation is written in the form of the point slope formula: $y = mx + b$ where m is the slope of the line and b is the y-axis intercept. For the given equation, $y = -3x - 3$, the slope of the line is negative 3 and the line intercepts the y-axis at negative 3. The graph in Figure 2 fits these criteria. The graph in Figure 1 intercepts the y-axis at positive 3. The graphs in Figure 3 and Figure 4 have slopes of positive 3.

10. A: The equation is written in the form $y = Ax^2 + B$ where A tells the concavity of the graph and B is the y- intercept. In this case, A equals negative 1. So the graph is concave down. B equals negative 5. So the graph intercepts the y-axis at negative 5. The graph in Figure 1 fits these criteria. The graph in Figure 2 intercepts the y-axis at positive 5. The graphs in Figure 3 and Figure 4 are concave up.

11. D: The list of coordinate pairs represents the x and y values of five points. The range is all the y values. Answer D contains all the y values of the coordinate pairs.

12. C: The list of coordinate pairs represents the x and y values of five points. The domain is all the x values. Answer C contains all the x values of the coordinate pairs.

13. C: Tyrone earns $10 per hour, and he works x number of hours. Therefore, he earns 10x for his time spent mowing a lawn. Furthermore, Tyrone charges an additional $10 for each lawn he mows. Therefore, his total earnings per lawn are calculated by: $y = 10x + 10$.

14. A: The graph that represents Tyrone's earnings per lawn can be determined from the equation $y = 10x + 10$, since Tyrone earns $10 for every x hours he spends mowing, with an additional overhead of $10 per job. This equation has a slope of 10. Furthermore, if Tyrone spends just 1 hour mowing a lawn, then he earns $20. The graph in Figure 1 fits these criteria.

15. B: Based on the definition of $A\theta B$,
$$1\theta 2 = (2)(1) + (3)(2) - 1 - 2$$
$$= 2 + 6 - 1 - 2$$
$$= 8 - 1 - 2$$
$$= 7 - 2$$
$$= 5$$

16. B: To factor the polynomial, find factors of the first and third term whose product can be added to get the middle term. Here, the factors 7 and -8 have a product of -56, and when added together yield -1. Another way to find the correct answer is to multiply the answer choices and select the choice that yields the original equation. In this case:
$$(x + 7)(x - 8) = (x)(x) + (x)(-8) + (7)(x) + (7)(-8)$$
$$= x^2 - 8x + 7x - 56$$
$$= x^2 - x - 56$$

17. D: The solution to the equation follows:
$$x^2 - 25 = 0$$
$$x^2 = 25$$
$$x = \sqrt{25}$$
$$x = +5 \text{ and } -5$$

18. C: To simplify the polynomial, group and combine all terms of the same order.
$$4x^3 + 5x - x^3 + 2x^2 + 17 - 3x^3 + 5x - 2x^2 + 3$$
$$(4x^3 - x^3 - 3x^3) + (2x^2 - 2x^2) + (5x + 5x) + (17 + 3)$$
$$0 + 0 + 10x + 20$$
$$10(x + 2)$$

19. B: A mathematical operation is commutative if altering the order does not alter the result of the operation. In other words, $a + b = b + a$, or $ab = ba$. Answer B fits this definition.

20. C: The distributive property says that terms inside a set of parentheses can be multiplied by a factor outside the parentheses. In other words, $a(b + c) = ab + ac$. Answer C fits this definition.

21. B: By definition, a linear function is a first degree polynomial function of one variable, and the data shown in Table 2 can be written as such. The variable is the number of hours practiced, and the score is a function of that variable.

22. A: In each case, the number of points scored (p) equals $3(h) + 2$ where h is the number of hours practiced. For example, $8 = (3)(2) + 2$ and $14 = (3)(4) + 2$. For answers C and D, the points scored are not written as functions of the hours practiced.

23. D: The range consists of all the values of the dependent variable. In this case, the dependent variable is the number of points scored.

24. C: The domain consists of all the values of the independent variable. In this case, the independent variable is the number of hours practiced.

25. B: The bar graph shown in Figure 2 is the only graph where the number of points scored corresponds to the number of hours practiced as presented in Table 2.

26. C: The slope of a line describes the change in the dependent variable divided by the change in the independent variable, i.e. the change in y over the change in x. To calculate the slope, consider any two points on the line. Let the first point be $(1, 14)$, and let the second point be $(2, 28)$.
$$\frac{y_2 - y_1}{x_2 - x_1} = \frac{28 - 14}{2 - 1} = \frac{14}{1} = 14$$

27. C: The slope of the line is the change in y divided by the change in x. Therefore, the units of the slope are the units of y over the units for x. The unit for y is the unit for distance or meters. The unit for x is the unit for time or seconds. Hence the units of the slope are meters over second or meters per second.

28. A: The slope describes the change in distance over the change in time. The change in distance over the change in time is a measure of the cheetah's speed in meters per second.

29. D: First write Equation A in slope-intercept form: $y = mx + b$ where b is the y-intercept and m is the slope:

$$10y - 5x = 40$$
$$10y = 5x + 40$$
$$y = 0.5x + 4$$

Based on the slope-intercept form of Equation A, the y-intercept $b = 4$, and the slope $m = 0.5$.

30. A: Write Equation B in slope-intercept form, $y = mx + b$:

$$10y - 10x = 20$$
$$10y = 10x + 20$$
$$y = x + 2$$

Based on the slope-intercept form of Equation B, the slope is 1, which is twice the slope of Equation A.

31. C: Based on the slope-intercept form of Equation B, the y-intercept is 2, which is half the y-intercept of Equation A.

32. B: The slope of a line is the change in y divided by the change in x. Calculate the slope as follows:

$$m = \frac{y_2 - y_1}{x_2 - x_1}$$
$$m = \frac{75 - 30}{8 - 3}$$
$$m = \frac{45}{5}$$
$$m = 9$$

33. D: Write the equation in slope-intercept form: $y = mx + b$ where m is the slope of the line and b is the y-intercept. In this case, the slope $m = 20$ and the y-intercept $b = 100$. Hence $y = 20x + 1000$.

34. A: At the intersection point of line 1 and line 2, $y_1 = y_2 = y$ and $x_1 = x_2 = x$. To find the x coordinate, let $y_1 = y_2$.

$$8x - 16 = -4x + 20$$
$$8x + 4x = 16 + 20$$
$$12x = 36$$
$$x = 3$$

Now find the y coordinate by substituting $x = 3$ into either the equation for line 1 or the equation for line 2:

$$y = -4x + 20$$
$$y = (-4)(3) + 20$$
$$y = -12 + 20$$
$$y = 8$$

Therefore, the point of intersection is $(3, 8)$.

35. B: The intersection point of line P and line Q will be common to both lines. See the explanation for question 34. Point (-9, -56) is the only point that is common to both lines.

36. A: Since Vivian will plant a total of 40 vegetables, the number of tomatoes plus the number of cucumbers is 40 or $T + C = 40$. Each tomato costs $1; so multiply the number of tomatoes by 1. Each cucumber costs $3; so multiply the number of cucumbers by 3. Vivian has a total of $80 to spend on tomatoes and cucumbers. So $T + 3C = 80$.

37. B: Use a linear system of equations to find the number of tomatoes. See the explanation for question 36. In this case, the system of equations is $T + C = 40$ and $T + 3C = 80$. Begin with $T + C = 40$ and solve for C:
$$T + C = 40$$
$$C = 40 - T$$
Now substitute the equation for C into the equation $T + 3C = 80$:
$$T + 3C = 80$$
$$T + 3(40 - T) = 80$$
$$T + 120 - 3T = 80$$
$$-2T = -40$$
$$T = 20$$
Therefore, Vivian will plant 20 tomato bushes in her garden.

38. B: Based on previous work, the number of tomatoes T = 20 and $T + C = 40$. Therefore, $C = 40 - 20 = 20$. Hence, Vivian will plant 20 cucumber bushes in her garden.

39. C: Despite the price difference, Vivian will purchase 20 tomatoes and 20 cucumbers. B and C are incorrect because no information is given about the space the vegetables require or Vivian's vegetable preference.

40. D: The new amount of space requires defining a new system of equations. Vivian will now plant a total of 50 vegetables. Hence:
$$T + C = 50$$
$$C = 50 - T$$
Therefore:
$$T + 3C = 80$$
$$T + 3(50 - T) = 80$$
$$T + 150 - 3T = 80$$
$$-2T = -70$$
$$T = 35$$

When she has more space, Vivian will plant 35 tomato bushes in her garden. Since $T + C = 50$, Vivian will plant 15 cucumber bushes in her garden.

41. A: In order to determine the number of questions Matthew must answer correctly, consider the number of points he must earn. Matthew will receive 3 points for each question he answers correctly, and x represents the number of questions. Therefore, Matthew will receive a total of 3x points for all the questions he answers correctly. Matthew must earn more than 96 points. Therefore, to determine the number of questions he must answer correctly, solve the inequality $3x > 96$.

42. C: First solve for the number of questions Matthew must answer correctly. See the explanation for question 41. To determine the number of correct answers Matthew needs, solve the following inequality:

$$3x > 96$$
$$x > \frac{96}{3}$$
$$x > 32$$

Therefore, Matthew must correctly answer at more than 32 questions to qualify for varsity sports. Since the test has 40 questions, he must answer less than 8 questions incorrectly. Matthew could also answer 0 questions incorrectly. Hence, the best inequality to describe the number of questions Matthew can answer incorrectly is $0 \leq x < 8$.

43. C: The inequality that best represents the number of questions Matthew can answer incorrectly is $0 \leq x < 8$. Hence, the left endpoint of the graph is 0, and the right endpoint is 8. Because Matthew can answer less than 8 questions incorrectly, the endpoint at 8 is not included in the data set and is represented by an open circle.

44. B: According to the statement of the problem, Matthew must earn more than 96 points. Therefore, answers C and D are incorrect. Furthermore, answer A is incorrect because this answer says his score can equal 96 points but Matthew needs more than 96 points. Because the test has a total of 40 questions, and each question is worth 3 points, Matthew can earn a maximum of $(3)(40)$ or 120 points. Hence the best inequality is $96 \leq p < 120$.

45. C: Answers A and B are incorrect because Matthew must earn more than 96 points, which means he must correctly answer more than 32 questions. Answer D is incorrect because the problem statement mentions nothing about Matthew's desire to work a part-time job.

46. D: The range is all the y values. Refer to a graph of y_1 shown below.

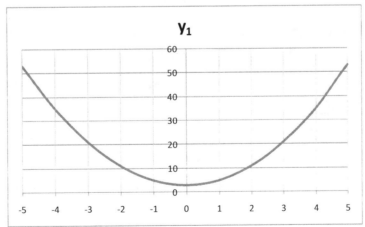

The minimum value for y is 3. Another way to solve this problem is to substitute the potential y values in the equation for y_1. For example,

$$y_1 = 2x^2 + 3$$
$$0 = 2x^2 + 3$$
$$-\frac{3}{2} = x^2$$

$$\sqrt{-\frac{3}{2}} = x$$

This statement has no real solution since it requires taking the square root of a negative number. Similar solutions are obtained if $y = 1$ or if $y = 2$.

47. B: The original function y_1 is concave up. See the graph of y_1 shown in the explanation for problem 46. Changing the coefficient of x^2 from +2 to -2 causes the function to be concave down. See the graph of y_2 shown below.

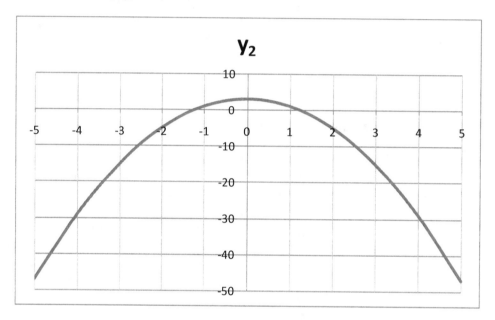

The y values for y_2 are different from those of y_1. Therefore, y_2 has a different range than y_1.

48. B: For function y_1, the y-intercept is +3. See the graph of y_1 shown in the explanation for problem 46. For function y_3, the y-intercept is -3. See the graph of y_3 shown below.

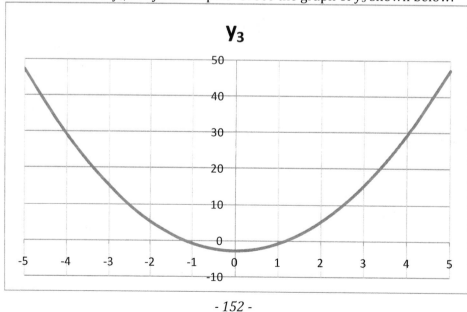

- 152 -

The graph of y_3 is similar to that of y_1 except the y-intercept of y_3 is 6 units below that of y_1. In other words, the difference between +3 and -3 is 6 units.

49. A: The graphs for y_1, y_2, and y_3 are displayed in the explanations for questions 46 – 48.

50. The correct answer is $x = -2$. The solution follows:
$$x^2 + 4x = -4$$
$$x^2 + 4x + 4 = 0$$
$$(x + 2)(x + 2) = 0$$
$$x + 2 = 0$$
$$x = -2$$

51. The correct answer is $x = -2$. The x-intercept is determined by setting the equation equal to zero and then solving for x. When $x^2 + 4x + 4 = 0$, then $x = -2$.

52. The correct answer is $x = -1$. The magnitude of x remains the same regardless of the power to which x is raised. Only 1 can be multiplied by itself several times and remain unchanged. The sign, however, alternates between positive and negative. Therefore, x must be -1. Note that multiplying a negative number by itself an even number of times yields a positive number. Multiplying a negative number by itself an odd number of times yields a negative number.

53. The correct answer is $x = -27$. The solution follows:
$$y = -\frac{1}{3}x$$
$$3y = -x$$
$$-3y = x$$
$$(-3)(9) = x$$
$$-27 = x$$

54. The correct answer is $x = 12$. The solution follows:
$$2^x = 4096$$
$$x \log 2 = \log 4096$$
$$x = \frac{\log 4096}{\log 2}$$
$$x = 12$$

Secret Key #1 - Time is Your Greatest Enemy

Pace Yourself

Wear a watch. At the beginning of the test, check the time (or start a chronometer on your watch to count the minutes), and check the time after every few questions to make sure you are "on schedule."

If you are forced to speed up, do it efficiently. Usually one or more answer choices can be eliminated without too much difficulty. Above all, don't panic. Don't speed up and just begin guessing at random choices. By pacing yourself, and continually monitoring your progress against your watch, you will always know exactly how far ahead or behind you are with your available time. If you find that you are one minute behind on the test, don't skip one question without spending any time on it, just to catch back up. Take 15 fewer seconds on the next four questions, and after four questions you'll have caught back up. Once you catch back up, you can continue working each problem at your normal pace.

Furthermore, don't dwell on the problems that you were rushed on. If a problem was taking up too much time and you made a hurried guess, it must be difficult. The difficult questions are the ones you are most likely to miss anyway, so it isn't a big loss. It is better to end with more time than you need than to run out of time.

Lastly, sometimes it is beneficial to slow down if you are constantly getting ahead of time. You are always more likely to catch a careless mistake by working more slowly than quickly, and among very high-scoring test takers (those who are likely to have lots of time left over), careless errors affect the score more than mastery of material.

Secret Key #2 - Guessing is not Guesswork

You probably know that guessing is a good idea. Unlike other standardized tests, there is no penalty for getting a wrong answer. Even if you have no idea about a question, you still have a 20-25% chance of getting it right.

Most test takers do not understand the impact that proper guessing can have on their score. Unless you score extremely high, guessing will significantly contribute to your final score.

Monkeys Take the Test

What most test takers don't realize is that to insure that 20-25% chance, you have to guess randomly. If you put 20 monkeys in a room to take this test, assuming they answered once per question and behaved themselves, on average they would get 20-25% of the questions correct. Put 20 test takers in the room, and the average will be much lower among guessed questions. Why?
    1. The test writers intentionally write deceptive answer choices that "look" right. A test

taker has no idea about a question, so he picks the "best looking" answer, which is often wrong. The monkey has no idea what looks good and what doesn't, so it will consistently be right about 20-25% of the time.

2. Test takers will eliminate answer choices from the guessing pool based on a hunch or intuition. Simple but correct answers often get excluded, leaving a 0% chance of being correct. The monkey has no clue, and often gets lucky with the best choice.

This is why the process of elimination endorsed by most test courses is flawed and detrimental to your performance. Test takers don't guess; they make an ignorant stab in the dark that is usually worse than random.

$5 Challenge

Let me introduce one of the most valuable ideas of this course—the $5 challenge:

You only mark your "best guess" if you are willing to bet $5 on it.
You only eliminate choices from guessing if you are willing to bet $5 on it.

Why $5? Five dollars is an amount of money that is small yet not insignificant, and can really add up fast (20 questions could cost you $100). Likewise, each answer choice on one question of the test will have a small impact on your overall score, but it can really add up to a lot of points in the end.

The process of elimination IS valuable. The following shows your chance of guessing it right:

If you eliminate wrong answer choices until only this many remain:	Chance of getting it correct:
1	100%
2	50%
3	33%

However, if you accidentally eliminate the right answer or go on a hunch for an incorrect answer, your chances drop dramatically—to 0%. By guessing among all the answer choices, you are GUARANTEED to have a shot at the right answer.

That's why the $5 test is so valuable. If you give up the advantage and safety of a pure guess, it had better be worth the risk.

What we still haven't covered is how to be sure that whatever guess you make is truly random. Here's the easiest way:

Always pick the first answer choice among those remaining.

Such a technique means that you have decided, **before you see a single test question**, exactly how you are going to guess, and since the order of choices tells you nothing about which one is correct, this guessing technique is perfectly random.

This section is not meant to scare you away from making educated guesses or eliminating choices; you just need to define when a choice is worth eliminating. The $5 test, along with a pre-defined random guessing strategy, is the best way to make sure you reap all of the benefits of guessing.

Secret Key #3 - Practice Smarter, Not Harder

Many test takers delay the test preparation process because they dread the awful amounts of practice time they think necessary to succeed on the test. We have refined an effective method that will take you only a fraction of the time.

There are a number of "obstacles" in the path to success. Among these are answering questions, finishing in time, and mastering test-taking strategies. All must be executed on the day of the test at peak performance, or your score will suffer. The test is a mental marathon that has a large impact on your future.

Just like a marathon runner, it is important to work your way up to the full challenge. So first you just worry about questions, and then time, and finally strategy:

Success Strategy

1. Find a good source for practice tests.
2. If you are willing to make a larger time investment, consider using more than one study guide. Often the different approaches of multiple authors will help you "get" difficult concepts.
3. Take a practice test with no time constraints, with all study helps, "open book." Take your time with questions and focus on applying strategies.
4. Take a practice test with time constraints, with all guides, "open book."
5. Take a final practice test without open material and with time limits.

If you have time to take more practice tests, just repeat step 5. By gradually exposing yourself to the full rigors of the test environment, you will condition your mind to the stress of test day and maximize your success.

Secret Key #4 - Prepare, Don't Procrastinate

Let me state an obvious fact: if you take the test three times, you will probably get three different scores. This is due to the way you feel on test day, the level of preparedness you have, and the version of the test you see. Despite the test writers' claims to the contrary, some versions of the test WILL be easier for you than others.

Since your future depends so much on your score, you should maximize your chances of success. In order to maximize the likelihood of success, you've got to prepare in advance.

This means taking practice tests and spending time learning the information and test taking strategies you will need to succeed.

Never go take the actual test as a "practice" test, expecting that you can just take it again if you need to. Take all the practice tests you can on your own, but when you go to take the official test, be prepared, be focused, and do your best the first time!

Secret Key #5 - Test Yourself

Everyone knows that time is money. There is no need to spend too much of your time or too little of your time preparing for the test. You should only spend as much of your precious time preparing as is necessary for you to get the score you need.

Once you have taken a practice test under real conditions of time constraints, then you will know if you are ready for the test or not.

If you have scored extremely high the first time that you take the practice test, then there is not much point in spending countless hours studying. You are already there.

Benchmark your abilities by retaking practice tests and seeing how much you have improved. Once you consistently score high enough to guarantee success, then you are ready.

If you have scored well below where you need, then knuckle down and begin studying in earnest. Check your improvement regularly through the use of practice tests under real conditions. Above all, don't worry, panic, or give up. The key is perseverance!

Then, when you go to take the test, remain confident and remember how well you did on the practice tests. If you can score high enough on a practice test, then you can do the same on the real thing.

Success Strategies

The most important thing you can do is to ignore your fears and jump into the test immediately. Do not be overwhelmed by any strange-sounding terms. You have to jump into the test like jumping into a pool—all at once is the easiest way.

Make Predictions

As you read and understand the question, try to guess what the answer will be. Remember that several of the answer choices are wrong, and once you begin reading them, your mind will immediately become cluttered with answer choices designed to throw you off. Your mind is typically the most focused immediately after you have read the question and digested its contents. If you can, try to predict what the correct answer will be. You may be surprised at what you can predict.

Quickly scan the choices and see if your prediction is in the listed answer choices. If it is, then you can be quite confident that you have the right answer. It still won't hurt to check the other answer choices, but most of the time, you've got it!

Answer the Question

It may seem obvious to only pick answer choices that answer the question, but the test writers can create some excellent answer choices that are wrong. Don't pick an answer just because it sounds right, or you believe it to be true. It MUST answer the question. Once you've made your selection, always go back and check it against the question and make sure that you didn't misread the question and that the answer choice does answer the question posed.

Benchmark

After you read the first answer choice, decide if you think it sounds correct or not. If it doesn't, move on to the next answer choice. If it does, mentally mark that answer choice. This doesn't mean that you've definitely selected it as your answer choice, it just means that it's the best you've seen thus far. Go ahead and read the next choice. If the next choice is worse than the one you've already selected, keep going to the next answer choice. If the next choice is better than the choice you've already selected, mentally mark the new answer choice as your best guess.

The first answer choice that you select becomes your standard. Every other answer choice must be benchmarked against that standard. That choice is correct until proven otherwise by another answer choice beating it out. Once you've decided that no other answer choice seems as good, do one final check to ensure that your answer choice answers the question posed.

Valid Information

Don't discount any of the information provided in the question. Every piece of information may be necessary to determine the correct answer. None of the information in the question is there to throw you off (while the answer choices will certainly have information to throw you off). If two seemingly unrelated topics are discussed, don't ignore either. You can be confident there is a relationship, or it wouldn't be included in the question, and you are probably going to have to determine what is that relationship to find the answer.

Avoid "Fact Traps"

Don't get distracted by a choice that is factually true. Your search is for the answer that answers the question. Stay focused and don't fall for an answer that is true but irrelevant. Always go back to the question and make sure you're choosing an answer that actually answers the question and is not just a true statement. An answer can be factually correct, but it MUST answer the question asked. Additionally, two answers can both be seemingly correct, so be sure to read all of the answer choices, and make sure that you get the one that BEST answers the question.

Milk the Question

Some of the questions may throw you completely off. They might deal with a subject you have not been exposed to, or one that you haven't reviewed in years. While your lack of knowledge about the subject will be a hindrance, the question itself can give you many clues that will help you find the correct answer. Read the question carefully and look for clues. Watch particularly for adjectives and nouns describing difficult terms or words that you don't recognize. Regardless of whether you completely understand a word or not, replacing it with a synonym, either provided or one you more familiar with, may help you to understand what the questions are asking. Rather than wracking your mind about specific detailed information concerning a difficult term or word, try to use mental substitutes that are easier to understand.

The Trap of Familiarity

Don't just choose a word because you recognize it. On difficult questions, you may not recognize a number of words in the answer choices. The test writers don't put "make-believe" words on the test, so don't think that just because you only recognize all the words in one answer choice that that answer choice must be correct. If you only recognize words in one answer choice, then focus on that one. Is it correct? Try your best to determine if it is correct. If it is, that's great. If not, eliminate it. Each word and answer choice you eliminate increases your chances of getting the question correct, even if you then have to guess among the unfamiliar choices.

Eliminate Answers

Eliminate choices as soon as you realize they are wrong. But be careful! Make sure you consider all of the possible answer choices. Just because one appears right, doesn't mean that the next one won't be even better! The test writers will usually put more than one good answer choice for every question, so read all of them. Don't worry if you are stuck between two that seem right. By getting down to just two remaining possible choices, your odds are now 50/50. Rather than wasting too much time, play the odds. You are guessing, but guessing wisely because you've been able to knock out some of the answer choices that you know are wrong. If you are eliminating choices and realize that the last answer choice you are left with is also obviously wrong, don't panic. Start over and consider each choice again. There may easily be something that you missed the first time and will realize on the second pass.

Tough Questions

If you are stumped on a problem or it appears too hard or too difficult, don't waste time. Move on! Remember though, if you can quickly check for obviously incorrect answer choices, your chances of guessing correctly are greatly improved. Before you completely give up, at least try to knock out a couple of possible answers. Eliminate what you can and then guess at the remaining answer choices before moving on.

Brainstorm

If you get stuck on a difficult question, spend a few seconds quickly brainstorming. Run through the complete list of possible answer choices. Look at each choice and ask yourself, "Could this answer the question satisfactorily?" Go through each answer choice and consider it independently of the others. By systematically going through all possibilities, you may find something that you would otherwise overlook. Remember though that when you get stuck, it's important to try to keep moving.

Read Carefully

Understand the problem. Read the question and answer choices carefully. Don't miss the question because you misread the terms. You have plenty of time to read each question thoroughly and make sure you understand what is being asked. Yet a happy medium must be attained, so don't waste too much time. You must read carefully, but efficiently.

Face Value

When in doubt, use common sense. Always accept the situation in the problem at face value. Don't read too much into it. These problems will not require you to make huge leaps of logic. The test writers aren't trying to throw you off with a cheap trick. If you have to go beyond creativity and make a leap of logic in order to have an answer choice answer the question, then you should look at the other answer choices. Don't overcomplicate the problem by creating theoretical relationships or explanations that will warp time or space. These are normal problems rooted in reality. It's just that the applicable relationship or explanation may not be readily apparent and you have to figure things out. Use your common sense to interpret anything that isn't clear.

Prefixes

If you're having trouble with a word in the question or answer choices, try dissecting it. Take advantage of every clue that the word might include. Prefixes and suffixes can be a huge help. Usually they allow you to determine a basic meaning. Pre- means before, post- means after, pro - is positive, de- is negative. From these prefixes and suffixes, you can get an idea of the general meaning of the word and try to put it into context. Beware though of any traps. Just because con- is the opposite of pro-, doesn't necessarily mean congress is the opposite of progress!

Hedge Phrases

Watch out for critical hedge phrases, led off with words such as "likely," "may," "can," "sometimes," "often," "almost," "mostly," "usually," "generally," "rarely," and "sometimes." Question writers insert these hedge phrases to cover every possibility. Often an answer choice will be wrong simply because it leaves no room for exception. Unless the situation calls for them, avoid answer choices that have definitive words like "exactly," and "always."

Switchback Words

Stay alert for "switchbacks." These are the words and phrases frequently used to alert you to shifts in thought. The most common switchback word is "but." Others include "although," "however," "nevertheless," "on the other hand," "even though," "while," "in spite of," "despite," and "regardless of."

New Information

Correct answer choices will rarely have completely new information included. Answer choices typically are straightforward reflections of the material asked about and will directly relate to the question. If a new piece of information is included in an answer choice that doesn't even seem to relate to the topic being asked about, then that answer choice is likely incorrect. All of the information needed to answer the question is usually provided for you in the question. You should not have to make guesses that are unsupported or choose answer choices that require unknown information that cannot be reasoned from what is given.

Time Management

On technical questions, don't get lost on the technical terms. Don't spend too much time on any one question. If you don't know what a term means, then odds are you aren't going to get much further since you don't have a dictionary. You should be able to immediately recognize whether or not you know a term. If you don't, work with the other clues that you have—the other answer choices and terms provided—but don't waste too much time trying to figure out a difficult term that you don't know.

Contextual Clues

Look for contextual clues. An answer can be right but not the correct answer. The contextual clues will help you find the answer that is most right and is correct. Understand the context in which a phrase or statement is made. This will help you make important distinctions.

Don't Panic

Panicking will not answer any questions for you; therefore, it isn't helpful. When you first see the question, if your mind goes blank, take a deep breath. Force yourself to mechanically go through the steps of solving the problem using the strategies you've learned.

Pace Yourself

Don't get clock fever. It's easy to be overwhelmed when you're looking at a page full of questions, your mind is full of random thoughts and feeling confused, and the clock is ticking down faster than you would like. Calm down and maintain the pace that you have set for yourself. As long as you are on track by monitoring your pace, you are guaranteed to have enough time for yourself. When you get to the last few minutes of the test, it may seem like you won't have enough time left, but if you only have as many questions as you should have left at that point, then you're right on track!

Answer Selection

The best way to pick an answer choice is to eliminate all of those that are wrong, until only one is left and confirm that is the correct answer. Sometimes though, an answer choice may immediately look right. Be careful! Take a second to make sure that the other choices are not equally obvious. Don't make a hasty mistake. There are only two times that you should stop before checking other answers. First is when you are positive that the answer choice you have selected is correct. Second is when time is almost out and you have to make a quick guess!

Check Your Work

Since you will probably not know every term listed and the answer to every question, it is important that you get credit for the ones that you do know. Don't miss any questions through careless mistakes. If at all possible, try to take a second to look back over your answer selection and make sure you've selected the correct answer choice and haven't made a costly careless mistake (such as marking an answer choice that you didn't mean to mark). The time it takes for this quick double check should more than pay for itself in caught mistakes.

Beware of Directly Quoted Answers

Sometimes an answer choice will repeat word for word a portion of the question or reference section. However, beware of such exact duplication. It may be a trap! More than likely, the correct choice will paraphrase or summarize a point, rather than being exactly the same wording.

Slang

Scientific sounding answers are better than slang ones. An answer choice that begins "To compare the outcomes..." is much more likely to be correct than one that begins "Because some people insisted..."

Extreme Statements

Avoid wild answers that throw out highly controversial ideas that are proclaimed as established fact. An answer choice that states the "process should used in certain situations, if..." is much more likely to be correct than one that states the "process should be discontinued completely." The first is a calm rational statement and doesn't even make a definitive, uncompromising stance, using a hedge word "if" to provide wiggle room, whereas the second choice is a radical idea and far more extreme.

Answer Choice Families

When you have two or more answer choices that are direct opposites or parallels, one of them is usually the correct answer. For instance, if one answer choice states "x increases" and another answer choice states "x decreases" or "y increases," then those two or three answer choices are very similar in construction and fall into the same family of answer choices. A family of answer choices consists of two or three answer choices, very similar in construction, but often with directly opposite meanings. Usually the correct answer choice will be in that family of answer choices. The "odd man out" or answer choice that doesn't seem to fit the parallel construction of the other answer choices is more likely to be incorrect.

Special Report: How to Overcome Test Anxiety

The very nature of tests caters to some level of anxiety, nervousness, or tension, just as we feel for any important event that occurs in our lives. A little bit of anxiety or nervousness can be a good thing. It helps us with motivation, and makes achievement just that much sweeter. However, too much anxiety can be a problem, especially if it hinders our ability to function and perform.

"Test anxiety," is the term that refers to the emotional reactions that some test-takers experience when faced with a test or exam. Having a fear of testing and exams is based upon a rational fear, since the test-taker's performance can shape the course of an academic career. Nevertheless, experiencing excessive fear of examinations will only interfere with the test-taker's ability to perform and chance to be successful.

There are a large variety of causes that can contribute to the development and sensation of test anxiety. These include, but are not limited to, lack of preparation and worrying about issues surrounding the test.

Lack of Preparation

Lack of preparation can be identified by the following behaviors or situations:

Not scheduling enough time to study, and therefore cramming the night before the test or exam
Managing time poorly, to create the sensation that there is not enough time to do everything
Failing to organize the text information in advance, so that the study material consists of the entire text and not simply the pertinent information
Poor overall studying habits

Worrying, on the other hand, can be related to both the test taker, or many other factors around him/her that will be affected by the results of the test. These include worrying about:

Previous performances on similar exams, or exams in general
How friends and other students are achieving
The negative consequences that will result from a poor grade or failure

There are three primary elements to test anxiety. Physical components, which involve the same typical bodily reactions as those to acute anxiety (to be discussed below). Emotional factors have to do with fear or panic. Mental or cognitive issues concerning attention spans and memory abilities.

Physical Signals

There are many different symptoms of test anxiety, and these are not limited to mental and emotional strain. Frequently there are a range of physical signals that will let a test taker know that he/she is suffering from test anxiety. These bodily changes can include the following:

Perspiring
Sweaty palms
Wet, trembling hands
Nausea
Dry mouth
A knot in the stomach
Headache
Faintness
Muscle tension
Aching shoulders, back and neck
Rapid heart beat
Feeling too hot/cold

To recognize the sensation of test anxiety, a test-taker should monitor him/herself for the following sensations:

The physical distress symptoms as listed above
Emotional sensitivity, expressing emotional feelings such as the need to cry or laugh too much, or a sensation of anger or helplessness
A decreased ability to think, causing the test-taker to blank out or have racing thoughts that are hard to organize or control.

Though most students will feel some level of anxiety when faced with a test or exam, the majority can cope with that anxiety and maintain it at a manageable level. However, those who cannot are faced with a very real and very serious condition, which can and should be controlled for the immeasurable benefit of this sufferer.

Naturally, these sensations lead to negative results for the testing experience. The most common effects of test anxiety have to do with nervousness and mental blocking.

Nervousness

Nervousness can appear in several different levels:

The test-taker's difficulty, or even inability to read and understand the questions on the test
The difficulty or inability to organize thoughts to a coherent form
The difficulty or inability to recall key words and concepts relating to the testing questions (especially essays)
The receipt of poor grades on a test, though the test material was well known by the test taker

Conversely, a person may also experience mental blocking, which involves:

Blanking out on test questions
Only remembering the correct answers to the questions when the test has already finished.

Fortunately for test anxiety sufferers, beating these feelings, to a large degree, has to do with proper preparation. When a test taker has a feeling of preparedness, then anxiety will be dramatically lessened.

The first step to resolving anxiety issues is to distinguish which of the two types of anxiety are being suffered. If the anxiety is a direct result of a lack of preparation, this should be considered a normal reaction, and the anxiety level (as opposed to the test results) shouldn't be anything to worry about. However, if, when adequately prepared, the test-taker still panics, blanks out, or seems to overreact, this is not a fully rational reaction. While this can be considered normal too, there are many ways to combat and overcome these effects.

Remember that anxiety cannot be entirely eliminated, however, there are ways to minimize it, to make the anxiety easier to manage. Preparation is one of the best ways to minimize test anxiety. Therefore the following techniques are wise in order to best fight off any anxiety that may want to build.

To begin with, try to avoid cramming before a test, whenever it is possible. By trying to memorize an entire term's worth of information in one day, you'll be shocking your system, and not giving yourself a very good chance to absorb the information. This is an easy path to anxiety, so for those who suffer from test anxiety, cramming should not even be considered an option.

Instead of cramming, work throughout the semester to combine all of the material which is presented throughout the semester, and work on it gradually as the course goes by, making sure to master the main concepts first, leaving minor details for a week or so before the test.

To study for the upcoming exam, be sure to pose questions that may be on the examination, to gauge the ability to answer them by integrating the ideas from your texts, notes and lectures, as well as any supplementary readings.

If it is truly impossible to cover all of the information that was covered in that particular term, concentrate on the most important portions, that can be covered very well. Learn these concepts as best as possible, so that when the test comes, a goal can be made to use these concepts as presentations of your knowledge.

In addition to study habits, changes in attitude are critical to beating a struggle with test anxiety. In fact, an improvement of the perspective over the entire test-taking experience can actually help a test taker to enjoy studying and therefore improve the overall experience. Be certain not to overemphasize the significance of the grade - know that the result of the test is neither a reflection of self worth, nor is it a measure of intelligence; one grade will not predict a person's future success.

To improve an overall testing outlook, the following steps should be tried:

Keeping in mind that the most reasonable expectation for taking a test is to expect to try to demonstrate as much of what you know as you possibly can.
Reminding ourselves that a test is only one test; this is not the only one, and there will be others.
The thought of thinking of oneself in an irrational, all-or-nothing term should be avoided at all costs.
A reward should be designated for after the test, so there's something to look forward to. Whether it be going to a movie, going out to eat, or simply visiting friends, schedule it in advance, and do it no matter what result is expected on the exam.

Test-takers should also keep in mind that the basics are some of the most important things, even beyond anti-anxiety techniques and studying. Never neglect the basic social, emotional and biological needs, in order to try to absorb information. In order to best achieve, these three factors must be held as just as important as the studying itself.

Study Steps

Remember the following important steps for studying:

Maintain healthy nutrition and exercise habits. Continue both your recreational activities and social pass times. These both contribute to your physical and emotional well being.
Be certain to get a good amount of sleep, especially the night before the test, because when you're overtired you are not able to perform to the best of your best ability.
Keep the studying pace to a moderate level by taking breaks when they are needed, and varying the work whenever possible, to keep the mind fresh instead of getting bored.
When enough studying has been done that all the material that can be learned has been learned, and the test taker is prepared for the test, stop studying and do something relaxing such as listening to music, watching a movie, or taking a warm bubble bath.

There are also many other techniques to minimize the uneasiness or apprehension that is experienced along with test anxiety before, during, or even after the examination. In fact, there are a great deal of things that can be done to stop anxiety from interfering with lifestyle and performance. Again, remember that anxiety will not be eliminated entirely, and it shouldn't be. Otherwise that "up" feeling for exams would not exist, and most of us depend on that sensation to perform better than usual. However, this anxiety has to be at a level that is manageable.

Of course, as we have just discussed, being prepared for the exam is half the battle right away. Attending all classes, finding out what knowledge will be expected on the exam, and knowing the exam schedules are easy steps to lowering anxiety. Keeping up with work will remove the need to cram, and efficient study habits will eliminate wasted time. Studying should be done in an ideal location for concentration, so that it is simple to become interested in the material and give it complete attention. A method such as SQ3R (Survey, Question, Read, Recite, Review) is a wonderful key to follow to make sure that the study habits are as effective as possible, especially in the case of learning from a textbook. Flashcards are great techniques for memorization. Learning to take good notes will mean that notes will be full of useful information, so that less sifting will need to be done to seek out what is pertinent for studying. Reviewing notes after class and then again on occasion will keep the information fresh in the mind. From notes that have been taken summary sheets and outlines can be made for simpler reviewing.

A study group can also be a very motivational and helpful place to study, as there will be a sharing of ideas, all of the minds can work together, to make sure that everyone understands, and the studying will be made more interesting because it will be a social occasion.

Basically, though, as long as the test-taker remains organized and self confident, with efficient study habits, less time will need to be spent studying, and higher grades will be achieved.

To become self confident, there are many useful steps. The first of these is "self talk." It has been shown through extensive research, that self-talk for students who suffer from test anxiety, should be well monitored, in order to make sure that it contributes to self confidence as opposed to sinking the student. Frequently the self talk of test-anxious students is negative or self-defeating, thinking that everyone else is smarter and faster, that they always mess up, and that if they don't do well, they'll fail the entire course. It is important to decreasing anxiety that awareness is made of self talk. Try writing any negative self thoughts and then disputing them with a positive statement instead. Begin self-encouragement as though it was a friend speaking. Repeat positive statements to help reprogram the mind to believing in successes instead of failures.

Helpful Techniques

Other extremely helpful techniques include:

Self-visualization of doing well and reaching goals
While aiming for an "A" level of understanding, don't try to "overprotect" by setting your expectations lower. This will only convince the mind to stop studying in order to meet the lower expectations.
Don't make comparisons with the results or habits of other students. These are individual factors, and different things work for different people, causing different results.
Strive to become an expert in learning what works well, and what can be done in order to improve. Consider collecting this data in a journal.
Create rewards for after studying instead of doing things before studying that will only turn into avoidance behaviors.
Make a practice of relaxing - by using methods such as progressive relaxation, self-hypnosis, guided imagery, etc - in order to make relaxation an automatic sensation.
Work on creating a state of relaxed concentration so that concentrating will take on the focus of the mind, so that none will be wasted on worrying.
Take good care of the physical self by eating well and getting enough sleep.
Plan in time for exercise and stick to this plan.

Beyond these techniques, there are other methods to be used before, during and after the test that will help the test-taker perform well in addition to overcoming anxiety.

Before the exam comes the academic preparation. This involves establishing a study schedule and beginning at least one week before the actual date of the test. By doing this, the anxiety of not having enough time to study for the test will be automatically eliminated. Moreover, this will make the studying a much more effective experience, ensuring that the learning will be an easier process. This relieves much undue pressure on the test-taker.

Summary sheets, note cards, and flash cards with the main concepts and examples of these main concepts should be prepared in advance of the actual studying time. A topic should never be eliminated from this process. By omitting a topic because it isn't expected to be on the test is only setting up the test-taker for anxiety should it actually appear on the exam. Utilize the course syllabus for laying out the topics that should be studied. Carefully go over the notes that were made in class, paying special attention to any of the issues that the professor took special care to emphasize while lecturing in class. In the textbooks, use the chapter review, or if possible, the chapter tests, to begin your review.

It may even be possible to ask the instructor what information will be covered on the exam, or what the format of the exam will be (for example, multiple choice, essay, free form, true-false). Additionally, see if it is possible to find out how many questions will be on the test. If a review sheet or sample test has been offered by the professor, make good use of it, above anything else, for the preparation for the test. Another great resource for getting to know the examination is reviewing tests from previous semesters. Use these tests to review, and aim to achieve a 100% score on each of the possible topics. With a few exceptions, the goal that you set for yourself is the highest one that you will reach.

Take all of the questions that were assigned as homework, and rework them to any other possible course material. The more problems reworked, the more skill and confidence will form as a result. When forming the solution to a problem, write out each of the steps. Don't simply do head work. By doing as many steps on paper as possible, much clarification and therefore confidence will be formed. Do this with as many homework problems as possible, before checking the answers. By checking the answer after each problem, a reinforcement will exist, that will not be on the exam. Study situations should be as exam-like as possible, to prime the test-taker's system for the experience. By waiting to check the answers at the end, a psychological advantage will be formed, to decrease the stress factor.

Another fantastic reason for not cramming is the avoidance of confusion in concepts, especially when it comes to mathematics. 8-10 hours of study will become one hundred percent more effective if it is spread out over a week or at least several days, instead of doing it all in one sitting. Recognize that the human brain requires time in order to assimilate new material, so frequent breaks and a span of study time over several days will be much more beneficial.

Additionally, don't study right up until the point of the exam. Studying should stop a minimum of one hour before the exam begins. This allows the brain to rest and put things in their proper order. This will also provide the time to become as relaxed as possible when going into the examination room. The test-taker will also have time to eat well and eat sensibly. Know that the brain needs food as much as the rest of the body. With enough food and enough sleep, as well as a relaxed attitude, the body and the mind are primed for success.

Avoid any anxious classmates who are talking about the exam. These students only spread anxiety, and are not worth sharing the anxious sentimentalities.

Before the test also involves creating a positive attitude, so mental preparation should also be a point of concentration. There are many keys to creating a positive attitude. Should fears become rushing in, make a visualization of taking the exam, doing well, and seeing an A written on the paper. Write out a list of affirmations that will bring a feeling of confidence, such as "I am doing well in my English class," "I studied well and know my material," "I enjoy this class." Even if the affirmations aren't believed at first, it sends a positive message to the subconscious which will result in an alteration of the overall belief system, which is the system that creates reality.

If a sensation of panic begins, work with the fear and imagine the very worst! Work through the entire scenario of not passing the test, failing the entire course, and dropping out of school, followed by not getting a job, and pushing a shopping cart through the dark alley where you'll live. This will place things into perspective! Then, practice deep breathing and create a visualization of the opposite situation - achieving an "A" on the exam, passing the entire course, receiving the degree at a graduation ceremony.

On the day of the test, there are many things to be done to ensure the best results, as well as the most calm outlook. The following stages are suggested in order to maximize test-taking potential:

Begin the examination day with a moderate breakfast, and avoid any coffee or beverages with caffeine if the test taker is prone to jitters. Even people who are used to managing caffeine can feel jittery or light-headed when it is taken on a test day.
Attempt to do something that is relaxing before the examination begins. As last minute cramming clouds the mastering of overall concepts, it is better to use this time to create a calming outlook.
Be certain to arrive at the test location well in advance, in order to provide time to select a location that is away from doors, windows and other distractions, as well as giving enough time to relax before the test begins.
Keep away from anxiety generating classmates who will upset the sensation of stability and relaxation that is being attempted before the exam.
Should the waiting period before the exam begins cause anxiety, create a self-distraction by reading a light magazine or something else that is relaxing and simple.

During the exam itself, read the entire exam from beginning to end, and find out how much time should be allotted to each individual problem. Once writing the exam, should more time be taken for a problem, it should be abandoned, in order to begin another problem. If there is time at the end, the unfinished problem can always be returned to and completed.

Read the instructions very carefully - twice - so that unpleasant surprises won't follow during or after the exam has ended.

When writing the exam, pretend that the situation is actually simply the completion of homework within a library, or at home. This will assist in forming a relaxed atmosphere, and will allow the brain extra focus for the complex thinking function.

Begin the exam with all of the questions with which the most confidence is felt. This will build the confidence level regarding the entire exam and will begin a quality momentum. This will also create encouragement for trying the problems where uncertainty resides.

Going with the "gut instinct" is always the way to go when solving a problem. Second guessing should be avoided at all costs. Have confidence in the ability to do well.

For essay questions, create an outline in advance that will keep the mind organized and make certain that all of the points are remembered. For multiple choice, read every answer, even if the correct one has been spotted - a better one may exist.

Continue at a pace that is reasonable and not rushed, in order to be able to work carefully. Provide enough time to go over the answers at the end, to check for small errors that can be corrected.

Should a feeling of panic begin, breathe deeply, and think of the feeling of the body releasing sand through its pores. Visualize a calm, peaceful place, and include all of the sights, sounds and sensations of this image. Continue the deep breathing, and take a few minutes to continue this with closed eyes. When all is well again, return to the test.

If a "blanking" occurs for a certain question, skip it and move on to the next question. There will be time to return to the other question later. Get everything done that can be done, first, to guarantee all the grades that can be compiled, and to build all of the confidence possible. Then return to the weaker questions to build the marks from there.

Remember, one's own reality can be created, so as long as the belief is there, success will follow. And remember: anxiety can happen later, right now, there's an exam to be written!

After the examination is complete, whether there is a feeling for a good grade or a bad grade, don't dwell on the exam, and be certain to follow through on the reward that was promised...and enjoy it! Don't dwell on any mistakes that have been made, as there is nothing that can be done at this point anyway.

Additionally, don't begin to study for the next test right away. Do something relaxing for a while, and let the mind relax and prepare itself to begin absorbing information again.

From the results of the exam - both the grade and the entire experience, be certain to learn from what has gone on. Perfect studying habits and work some more on confidence in order to make the next examination experience even better than the last one.

Learn to avoid places where openings occurred for laziness, procrastination and day dreaming.

Use the time between this exam and the next one to better learn to relax, even learning to relax on cue, so that any anxiety can be controlled during the next exam. Learn how to relax the body. Slouch in your chair if that helps. Tighten and then relax all of the different muscle groups, one group at a time, beginning with the feet and then working all the way up to the neck and face. This will ultimately relax the muscles more than they were to begin with. Learn how to breathe deeply and comfortably, and focus on this breathing going in and out as a relaxing thought. With every exhale, repeat the word "relax."

As common as test anxiety is, it is very possible to overcome it. Make yourself one of the test-takers who overcome this frustrating hindrance.

Additional Bonus Material

Due to our efforts to try to keep this book to a manageable length, we've created a link that will give you access to all of your additional bonus material.

Please visit http://www.mometrix.com/bonus948/gaalgebra to access the information.